The Asbury Theological Seminary Series in Christian Revitalization Studies

This volume is published in collaboration with the Center for the Study of World Christian Revitalization Movements, a cooperative initiative of Asbury Theological Seminary faculty. Building on the work of the previous Wesleyan/Holiness Studies Center at the Seminary, the Center provides a focus for research in the Wesleyan Holiness and other related Christian renewal movements, including Pietism and Pentecostal movements, which have had a world impact. The research seeks to develop analytical models of these movements, including their biblical and theological assessment. Using an interdisciplinary approach, the Center bridges relevant discourses in several areas in order to gain insights for effective Christian mission globally. It recognizes the need for conducting research that combines insights from the history of evangelical renewal and revival movements with anthropological and religious studies literature on revitalization movements. It also networks with similar or related research and study centers around the world, in addition to sponsoring its own research projects.

In this study, *Ecology of Evangelism: Trinity, Communication, and Systems*, Sunil Kim presents an interrelated (ecological) model of evangelism within the context of Trinitarian theology. He does so with reference to a methodology which provides insight to the various ways of doing evangelism by highlighting their relationship with other church practices. It is a field tested approach, which facilitates the advancement of research in understanding Christian revitalization movements. The "perichoretic" relationship implicit in Trinitarian thought provides a theological point of reference for this study . To that end, we present this title as an innovative contribution to our series in the study of Christian revitalization movements.

    J. Steven O'Malley
    General Editor
    The Asbury Theological Seminary Studies in World Christian Revitalization

Sub-Series Foreword
Intercultural Studies

Modernization in the history of the West has brought Fordism: assembly line production based on uniformity, specialization, and efficiency. In some ways, the church has emulated these business styles in organization and programs. This has led to what Sunil Kim calls a "narrow view" of evangelism, a practice separated from the other functions of the church. Kim wisely goes back to the beginning, appropriating an economic understanding of the Trinity as the basis for evangelism (and mission). He thus avoids the monadic (one person speaking) and even dyadic (one person speaking to another person) mindset in favor of a holistic or "ecological" understanding of evangelism in a complex system of relationships emanating from the Trinity to the world. The Trinity reaches out to the whole of the Trinity's Creation; the evangelism of humans is a subset of this complex salvation system.

Kim considers various theories of evangelism as well as explores a variety of contextual issues that may contribute to the success or failure of a church's evangelism efforts. He draws on theology, the social sciences, particularly communication theory, as well as evangelism theory. For example, one thrust of communication theory is the notion of "media ecology" (Marshall McLuhan), the study of all factors, including the media through which evangelism takes place. Indeed, if "the medium IS the message," then the message, as a propositional statement, is not the message. Kim's work is a timely reminder that replicating someone else's evangelism methods for one's own church or denomination does not guarantee the same success. An *Ecology of Evangelism* firmly grounded in the Trinity opens the way to an ecologically embedded evangelism.

Michael A. Rynkiewich
Editor for the sub-series on Intercultural Studies

Ecology of Evangelism

Trinity, Communication, and Systems

Sunil Kim

*The Asbury Theological Seminary Series in
World Christian Revitalization Movements in Intercultural Studies*

EMETH PRESS
www.emethpress.com

Ecology of Evangelism: Trinity, Communication, and Systems

Copyright © 2016 Sunil Kim

Printed in the United States of America on acid-free paper

All rights reserved. No part of this book may be reproduced, or stored in a retrieval system or transmitted in any form or by any means, electronic, mechanical, photocopying, recording, scanning or otherwise, except as permitted by the 1976 United States Copyright Act, or with the prior written permission of Emeth Press. Requests for permission should be addressed to: Emeth Press, P. O. Box 23961, Lexington, KY 40523-3961.

http://www.emethpress.com.

Library of Congress Cataloging-in-Publication Data

Names: Kim, Sunil, author.
Title: Ecology of evangelism : trinity, communication, and systems / Sunil Kim.
Description: Lexington : Emeth Press, 2016. | Series: The Asbury Theological Seminary series in intercultural studies | Includes bibliographical references.
Identifiers: LCCN 2016040918 | ISBN 9781609471033 (alk. paper)
Subjects: LCSH: Evangelistic work. | Missions--Theory. | Trinity. | Communication--Religious aspects--Christianity. | Ecology--Philosophy. | Ecology--Religious aspects.
Classification: LCC BV3793 .K39 2016 | DDC 269/.2--dc23
LC record available at https://lccn.loc.gov/2016040918

Table of Contents

Introduction / 1

Chapter One / 9
The Foundational Phase: A Trinitarian Vision for an Ecology of Evangelism / 9
    The Conceptual Significance of the Trinity / 9
    Anthropological Significance of the Trinitarian Theology / 14
    Communicative Significance of Trinitarian Theology / 19
    Summary / 26

Chapter Two / 29
The Descriptive Phase: The Mechanistic Domination of Communication and Evangelism / 29
    The Underlying Worldview of the Technological Culture / 29
    Modern Technological Culture and Its Impact Upon Communication / 32
    Communication Practices Shaped by Technology / 34
    Assessment of Evangelism Shaped by Technological Culture / 41
    Concluding Assessment / 52

Chapter Three / 55
The Investigative Phase: Alternative Thinking in Ecological Terms / 55
    Ecological Worldview / 55
    Applications of Ecological Epistemology / 60
    Conclusion: Benefits and Limitations of Ecological Thinking / 66

Chapter Four / 69
The Correlative Phase: Conversion and Christian Communication / 69
    Conversion and Spiritual Development / 70
    Conversion and Spiritual Development as an Ecological Process / 75
    Summary / 82

Chapter Five / 83
The Strategic Phase: Ecological Systems of EvangelismSystems Thinking and Evangelism / 83
  Microsystem and Evangelism / 85
  Mesosystem and Evangelism / 92
  Exosystem and Evangelism / 101
  Macrosystem and Evangelism / 111
  Chronosystem and Evangelism / 114
  A Narrative Application of Ecological Systems: *Hitsujigaoka* / 116

Conclusion / 123
The Trinitarian Consummation of Ecological Systems for Evangelism / 123

Bibliography / 125

Introduction

This book outlines an approach to the method and understanding of evangelism, an approach which I term the "trinitarian ecology for witness." The juxtaposition of "trinitarian" and "ecology" is meant to promote an interrelated model of evangelistic communication within the purview of Trinitarian theology. The word ecology is derived from the Greek oikos, meaning "household." The concept of ecology in biological terms refers to a system of organisms' interaction with environments. In more recent usage, it also has come to refer to a methodological tool which accounts for the impact of various disciplines and systems in a given reality. It is this latter application of the ecological idea, which is of interest here. Here, it will be accorded "its fullest possible extension as an exhaustive inquiry into the vast and intricate pattern that is, in nature, the study of the relation of each thing to everything else."[1] In tune with this line of thought, the concept of ecology can be defined as the investigation of the relationship between religion and its natural environment in the study of religious phenomenon.

The ecological vision of reality brings insight to the various ways of doing evangelism by highlighting their interrelationship with other church practices. There is a tendency to approach evangelism myopically as a program or as a special activity in a church. Those who are interested in evangelism tend to be interested only in gaining knowledge of evangelistic programs to be used on the spot and tend to disregard the larger context of the church. It is to this narrow view of evangelism that the ecological approach might be a helpful corrective. But the ecological approach should not be a self-referenced project of evangelism. The Trinitarian manifestations will do justice to the reciprocal relationship of each member with other, the so-called "perichoretic" relationship. It is in the dynamic coexistence that the triune God enters into relationship with humanity and humanity is called upon to reflect this character of relationship. Therefore, as the title connotes, I mean to emphasize the Trinitarian theology as conditioning, grounding, and setting the range of ecological implications.

---

[1] Amos H. Hawley, *Human Ecology: A Theory of Community Structure* (New York: Ronald Press, 1950), 9.

Assessing the Issue

To get a better sense of the evangelistic field, I interviewed several pastors who actively engage in planning and implementing evangelism programs. Chief among them are the cases of two contrasting churches in practicing evangelism and garnering its fruits contrary to conventional expectations.[2] Pastor Min of the Lighthouse Church (pseudonyms) has been in charge of evangelism programs for the whole congregation. Lighthouse Church is a Korean immigrant congregation on the outskirts of Los Angeles. As a newly planted church, it has grown rapidly in just a few years with its total number approaching 1000 members. But its initial growth has more recently encountered stagnation. In order to spark the growth of the church again, pastor Min was active in learning and introducing updated evangelism programs such as Alpha and "Customized Evangelism." While Alpha is more targeted to the postmodern generation, "Customized Evangelism" has its origin in the Korean context and is tailored to the various needs of specific generations or particular genders. The Lighthouse Church has held events and small group gatherings according to the recommendations of the curriculum. But pastor Min confessed that the church appeared to have implemented these new evangelistic methods to no avail. There is no apparent evidence that the recent new members joined the church in relation to those updated evangelistic programs.

Another case is found in a church which has made great strides in attracting new members--particularly among the younger generation. Pastor Sohn was in charge of the ministry department for young adults at Young-san church in the south east of Korea. This particular area was less evangelized than any other parts in Korea. The church had been steadily growing when pastor Sohn joined the leadership team. But the ministry to young adults had been the least successful among all the ministries in the church. During his five years in ministry, the young adult group has increased from fifteen to more than two hundred members. More than eighty percent of the new members were from a non-Christian background. A more startling fact is that pastor Sohn has been using quite traditional evangelism methods--such as Four Spiritual Laws and Evangelism Explosion in drawing the younger generation. The effective ministry of Young-san church's young adults group was even named as one of the most successful cases of evangelism by the Korean Campus Crusade for Christ.

What conclusions can be made from the above two cases? Do they prove that a certain evangelistic method should be preferred above another? Or do we need to rediscover the value of more traditional evangelism methods? There are numerous variables apart from evangelism program itself to ex-

---

[2]The following accounts are based on my interviews with the two directors of evangelism who provided me with a personal evaluation of their evangelism activities of their respective churches. All names of persons and churches are fictional.

plain the above results such as leadership issues, church location, and the level of outreach training in the congregations. However, despite these variables, at some level we tend to expect that effective evangelism is a function of programs that are well-crafted and carefully tailored to the specific needs of a target audience. While we focus on the mechanistic application of the proved evangelism programs, it is likely that we may miss the environmental factors that surround evangelistic activities. The churches expend their efforts in finding newly developed models of evangelism rather than looking at the overall fabric into which the variety of activities and elements of the congregation are weaved. This tendency causes the church to miss the interrelatedness of other church activities with evangelistic efforts, and eventually lose the evangelistic potential in holistic terms. To account for the contextual components that may interact with evangelistic methodologies, we need a more organic framework to analyze the process of how evangelism takes place. This framework allows us to see that what counts is the way which we approach evangelism, not the particular program we employ for effective witness to the gospel. This study deals with the matter of attitude, or worldview underlying our evangelistic activities by challenging the program-oriented notion of evangelistic communication and proposing the ecological view of evangelistic systems.

Embedded in the program-centered approach to evangelism is the technological mindset, which, in turn, grew out of the mechanistic worldview of the Western epistemological tradition. As an alternative to such a technological, mechanistic worldview that has affected evangelism, I propose an ecological approach to understanding evangelism. It is my premise that the whole of creation (including human beings) is interrelated in reflection of the self-relatedness of the Trinity. Also, the redemptive work of the triune God in history is carried out in like fashion with the interrelated cooperation between the three divine persons. This theological vision grounds the ecological worldview. Specifically, the concept of ecology provides a larger framework within which the complex relations between communication, culture, and evangelism may be analyzed. This fresh approach to evangelism from an ecological perspective will help the church overcome the single-minded approach to evangelism which focuses only on the direct communication of the gospel. And it will help the church consider the various potential inherent in the life of the church as well as rediscover the evangelistic value of all church activities and practices in a systemic form. The thrust of this study is, therefore, to document and delineate promising lines of research on the influence of ecological systems that affect the capacity of evangelistic communication.

Approaches to the Issue

The overall methodology of this study will proceed on the basis of practical theology, which investigates and reflects the praxis of the church. Practical theology by its very nature is an interdisciplinary activity[3], that is, it is eclectic, drawing from various disciplines. Thus this study incorporates insights from various fields within the theological arena: church history, theology, biblical studies--which are all important. This study will also need to draw upon insights from the social sciences--psychology, sociology, cultural studies, and communication theory. All this will be blended together in a coherent way to establish an ecological framework for understanding and practicing evangelism. Thus it will be integrative--using various sources for setting forth a plausible and practical case for the praxis of the church.

The working definition of evangelism in this study is closely bound up with the communicative aspect of evangelism. Already there are a number of judicious approaches to defining evangelism within a theological enterprise. Evangelism has been understood as "initiating people into the reign of the Kingdom,"[4] or "initiating people into the Christian discipleship."[5] While appreciating such attempts to lay out the theological significance of evangelism in the whole scheme of Christian life, this study narrows its focus to the communicative aspects of evangelism. Thus, here evangelism is defined as "a communicative effort in the whole area of life to help people enter the Christian faith in radical allegiance to the Lordship of Christ." This working definition of evangelism has legitimacy on the basis of the fact that communication is at the heart of evangelistic activity and conversion constitutes the crucial component of evangelism.

The term communication also can be used in various ways. One study of communication may investigate the process of how a message is transmitted through any media to the receiver. A rhetorical study of communication may focus on the essential components for persuasion to take place. Basically, human communication encompasses a wide array of interaction between human beings. The so-called "media ecology" developed by Marshall McLuhan is the study of the roles that symbols and the various media of communication play in the complex systems of human culture. The scope of communication we will be considering is far wider than is usually expected in the media ecology. All human behavior including non-verbal communication functions as communicative action. The cultural form in which the whole area of human life engages has a communicative dimension and conveys a certain message.

My premise is that our evangelistic activities inherently involve more than just propositional messages and include artistic senses and everyday life values that are so organically inter-related that these aspects may get the Christian message across better than transmitting the content of the message

---

[3] Paul Ballard and John Pritchard, *Practical Theology in Action: Christian Thinking in the Service of Church and Society* (London: SPCK, 1996), 104.

[4] William Abraham, *The Logic of Evangelism* (Grand Rapids: Eerdmans, 1989), 95.

[5] Scott J. Jones, *The Evangelistic Love of God and Neighbor: A Theology of Witness & Discipleship* (Nashville: Abingdon, 2003), 114-116.

itself. Thus all spheres of communication function in a synchronized pattern, which I call an ecological process of evangelism. In exploring the plural dimensions of evangelistic communication in particular, I perceive the need for a more organic approach to multi-sensory resources for evangelism.

It is necessary here to distinguish "ecological" from "holistic," (which is more familiar term) as we address issues in evangelism and missions. Both concepts share many commonalities, in that both see the reality of both the context and its totality. There is, however, a significant difference between the two. A holistic view sees its object as a whole, while an ecological worldview goes beyond looking only at something as a whole but also explores how this whole is embedded into larger wholes and how different parts of the whole affect each other in an interrelated way.[6]

The holistic view of a computer, for example, would imply seeing monitor, keyboard, mouse, and main body altogether but independently. The ecological view of a computer would focus on the functional interrelatedness of all its parts and also ask a question like, "What is the effect on marriage life of having a computer at home?" or "Where does the screen come from and how will its mass production affect the environment?" An ecological view, understood in this way, embeds the whole in a dialogue with the other or larger wholes.

Ecological systems theory helps us examine the plural and interrelated dimensions of evangelistic communication, since an ecological perspective looks at numerous variables that are intertwined around the process of human development on which conversion crucially impinges. Urie Bronfenbrenner broke ground by asserting that human development does not take place solely in a cause-effect structure and by examining human development in context. He repeatedly insists that human development takes place in the interactions of five eco-systems: microsystem, mesosystem, exosystem, macrosystem, and chronosystem. Microsystem is defined as the immediate setting which the individual faces. Mesosystem is described as the relationship between microsystems. Exosystem is used to describe the influences on the individual over which he or she has no control. Macrosystem involves the culture, ideology, and attitude that individuals share. The last system Bronfenbrenner articulated was the "chronosystem" which encompasses the evolving interconnected nature of the person and environment over time.[7] This system involves the patterning of environment events and transitions over the life course as well as socio-historical circumstances. This study will be an

---

[6] I am indebted for this insight to the conversation between Fritjof Capra and David Steindal-Rast. See Fritjof Capra and David Steindal-Rast with Thomas Matus, *Belonging to the Universe: Explorations on the Frontiers of Science & Spirituality* (New York: HarperCollins, 1991), 69-70.

[7] Urie Bronfenbrenner, "Ecological Systems Theory," in Ross Vasta ed., *Six Theories of Child Development: Revised Formulations and Current Issues* (Greenwich, CT: JAI Press, 1989), 187-250.

attempt to explore the possibility that the interactive structure of these five systems can be applied in unraveling the communicative process and effect of evangelism.

However, ecology is not the end of the whole story. Ecological process is also in the creative and redemptive framework of the triune God. Those ecological systems must be in constant communion with the Trinitarian work. This theological vision will be the all-encompassing and underlying theme that runs throughout this study.

Beginning with these preliminary thoughts on evangelistic communication within the paradigm of the Trinitarian ecology, the discussion henceforth will be organized into five phases: foundational, descriptive, investigative, correlative, and strategic. This sequence builds on and modifies Don Browning's model of exploring fundamental practical theology. He sets forth the sequential steps of proposing a practical theology: describing the existential situation, exploring practical wisdom and theological understanding, and, finally, proposing a strategy when we come to deal with the practical agenda in a practical theological way.[8] His underlying assumption is that theology moves from practice to theory and then back to practice.[9] Thus his practical theology begins with practical concerns, explores practical wisdom from theology, and eventually attempts to offer practical strategies to those concerns. While Browning explores practical wisdom to assess practical situations first and then presents theology to answer to the problems, this study seeks to critically modify Browning's model by paying attention to the particularly Trinitarian implications for theory and practice in the forefront of my argument. I will begin by articulating the theological grounds for addressing practical concerns, because the Trinitarian way of being is the *raison d'etre* for all creation in the Christian tradition. The theological vision of the Trinity does not merely provide the matrix for the existence of creation but also holds a prospect for restoration of the whole universe. Thus the Trinitarian framework will ground, validate, and drive the ecological process of evangelistic communication throughout this study.

Chapter one is the foundational phase in which this study seeks to find theological justification for an ecological perception of Christian practice. It inquires into our sense of the world and our self-identity. Trinitarian theology provides the holistic understanding of humanity and creation, and this also leads to an emphasis on the multifaceted mode of communication in accordance with the way in which the divine persons interact as well as the way the triune God approaches humans in history. This integrative and eclectic description of Trinitarian discourse will serve as the foundation for specifica-

---

[8] Don S. Browning, *A Fundamental Practical Theology: Descriptive and Strategic Proposals* (Minneapolis: Fortress, 1991), 5-9. Throughout the book Browning adopts this sequence of logic to grapple with the practical issues of the sample churches he focuses.

[9] Ibid., 9.

tion of ecological systems for evangelism and clothe the subsequent discussion with the Trinitarian paradigm.

In the light of a theological foundation for ecology and communication, chapter two will serve as a "descriptive phase" which wrestles with the question of what is wrong in our understanding of humanity and nature, and our approach to evangelism. It will do this by describing the mechanistic mode of worldview in a philosophical perspective with its consequent forms of communication.

Chapter three as an "investigative phase" is an attempt to explore how an organic worldview has emerged in response to the mechanistic view of the world and human life. This chapter will investigate the key figures to be noted with respect to constructing the idea of an ecological communication in response to such mechanistic dualism. Urie Bronfenbrenner makes an innovative case that human development takes place in the interrelated web of ecological settings. Bronfenbrenner's systems model will lay the foundation for further development of ecological evangelism in a practical way.

Chapter four is devoted to constructing a "correlative phase"[10] by construing conversion as ecological development and widening the dimensions of Christian communication. In order to adopt the ecology of human development model in evangelism, it will be necessary first to spell out religious conversion in terms of human development. Thus this chapter will articulate the relationship between conversion and human development while attempting to establish conversion as a critical part of spiritual development which brings about a radical transformation of the quality of human development.

The strategic phase of this study will consist of presenting foundational ideas for practice and exemplary cases that find an ecological approach to evangelism to be viable for Christian practice. In doing so, this study will build on Bronfenbrenner's five systems of ecological impact on human development. Sustained attempts will be made to articulate evangelistic models which are commensurate with the micro-, meso-, exo-, macro-, and, most recently, chrono-systems in the way human development takes place.

It will also be noted by way of conclusion that ecological systems do not govern the whole process of evangelistic communication in an autonomous way. As the ecological view posits all phenomena in interconnection with the larger whole, these five systems must be subjugated with constant reference to the Trinitarian work in history. With this awareness, I will summarize the ecological systems approach to evangelism in the theological vision of the Trinitarian economy.

---

[10]The correlative phase is added to the model of practical theological study set forth by Browning. I am indebted in using that term to Browning's discussion of Tillich and Tracy's use of correlation to present a theological task that answers existential questions emerged from cultural experiences in a critical dialogue between theology and culture. See Browning, 44-47.

Chapter One

Foundational Phase: A Trinitarian Vision for an Ecology of Evangelism

Evangelism is grounded in the practical dimension of theological activity and must be presented pragmatically, but it is important that it be theologically and philosophically articulated as well. Without an underpinning of firm biblical and theological foundations, evangelism can soon deteriorate into shallow pragmatism. The aim of the present chapter is to seek a theological paradigm that addresses human existence and communication, which ultimately leads to the ecological vision of evangelism.

The ways in which a particular theology engages with practical concerns can vary according a theological tradition. If a theological worldview provides a total framework for the way in which we understand human thought and behavior, it must be posited at the forefront. Trinitarian thinking is central to Christian theology. We confess our devotion to the One who is the ground of all being, the One who is most vividly revealed in the concrete and embodied Jesus, and the One whom we experience as a living, present reality. This chapter will also attempt to discern the communicative aspects of Trinitarian theology by spelling out practical implications with reference to the ecological nature of human beings. The discussion here will bring key insights to evangelistic communication by recapitulating some of the practical aspects of the Trinity. The present chapter will seek a theological foundation for an ecological view of humanity and an interrelated mode of evangelistic communication.

The Conceptual Significance of the Trinity

It is widely accepted among theologians that Karl Barth reestablished the importance of the doctrine of the Trinity in the twentieth century. For Barth, the Trinity is the answer we get when we come to the Scriptures and inquire about the essential nature of God.

The name Father, Son, and Spirit means that God is the one God in a threefold repetition; and that in such a way, that this repetition itself is grounded in His Godhead; but also in such a way that only in this repetition is He the one God; in such a way that His Godhead stands or falls with the fact that in this repetition He is God; but also precisely for the reason that in each repetition He is the one God.[11]

In *Church Dogmatics,* he articulates the connection between the Trinitarian approach and the work of Christ, "The Trinitarian God revealed in Jesus Christ is a God who desires to enter into communion with human beings in his love."[12] This notion of Trinitarian movement postulates the premise that Christian theology must always speak about God on the basis of God's self-communication in Christ and in the Spirit. At this juncture, how the triune God exists and interacts within Godself needs to be established in order to apply Trinitarian theology to Christian practice.

Simultaneousness of the One and the Many

Despite its placement at the center of the creeds throughout history, the doctrine of the Trinity has not been given its due place in Christian theology. The concept of God among Christian theologians has tended to drift towards monotheism rather than attempting to theologically affirm the plural nature of God in unity.

In the church, it was the Cappadocian Fathers who first stressed relation over substance as the primary mode of divine existence.[13] The focus on substance has generated confusion with regard to our understanding of the Trinity. The notion of three persons and one being was hard to grasp in terms of substance. Human endeavors to articulate the three-ness of one being in a substantial way have not been adequately persuasive. The Cappadocian theologians and other Greek Orthodox theologians made a significant contribution to this thorny area of theological inquiry by considering the doctrine of the Trinity from a relational perspective. The relational perspective of the Trinity sheds some lights on the way in which we perceive the reality today.

Epistemological insight into understanding three-ness in one has been set forth by Colin Gunton in his book *The One, the Three and the Many*. Gunton argues, throughout the book, that the modern way of thinking has engendered alienation between singularity and plurality, or (in his terms) one and many. The confusion stems from thinking that the subject can exist sufficiently alone without reference to its environment. He also suggests that we will not understand our place in the world unless we face up to the way in which

---

[11]Karl Barth, *Church Dogmatics*, Vol. I:1, trans. G. W. Bromiley (Edinburgh: T&T Clark, 1970), 402.

[12]Karl Barth, *Church Dogmatics*, Vol. III:2, trans. Harold Knight *et al.* (Edinburgh: T&T Clark, 1969), 288.

[13]Catherine M. LaCugna, *God for US: The Trinity and Christian Life* (San Francisco: Harper/Collins, 1991), 54.

we are internally related to the rest of the world.[14] Gunton traces the root of this false dichotomy back to two polarized ancient Greek philosophers, Heraclitus and Parmenides. Heraclitus gave priority to the many over the one by insisting that everything that exists is in flux and does not remain the same. There are plural entities and incessant motions in such a way that he advocated the many over the one. Parmenides takes the opposite position. He believed that reality is timeless, universal, and unchanging. There is a universal one which underlies the many--who do not really exist, but rather appear.[15]

According to Gunton, the debate between the one and the many has pervaded Western thought down through the ages in shaping our understanding of "who we are and the world in which we are set."[16] Priority of the one over the many has led to overriding emphasis on a single factor with which we approach the truth. Gunton argues that this particularity or loss of relationality in emphasis on the one has led to an essentially rationalist conception of human beings.

> The reduction of the many to the one . . . means a tendency to conceive the rational capacities of the human being at the expense of other dimensions of being, especially the aesthetic and material. We truly are when we think, but not when we love or make music. And that leads us to the second dimension of Hellenistic philosophy's problematic legacy, the rationalizing of the human relation to the rest of the world.[17]

In a response to this universalizing tendency of the one, Gunton regards the arts as being significant, since "they mark an important aspect of what we make of the particular things in the world."[18] Humans engage with the sensible and material world at various points in different ways. What we feel from viewing an art work or listening to a song can greatly vary. "The results of human craft or art are particular: the outcome of engagement with the material world in all its brute particularity and intractability."[19] The many unfolds more avenues through which we experience the world and approach reality.

Christian theology has long held that God is one in being and three in persons. The confusion and improbability about the duality of particularity and universality stem from a failure to recognize God, the One, as the focus of the unity of all things.[20] The confession that God exists as a triune being leads us to re-conceive the created order in light of the mystery of concurrence between the one and the many. This is because the creation bears the mark of its creator and, especially, because human beings are made in the

---

[14]Colin Gunton, *The One, The Three and The Many: God, Creation and the Culture of Modernity* (Cambridge, England: Cambridge University Press, 2002), Introduction.
[15]Ibid., 17-18.
[16]Ibid., 6.
[17]Ibid., 49-50.
[18]Ibid., 50.
[19]Ibid.
[20]Ibid., 38.

image of the Creator. Thus, attention to the triune nature of God will help us rethink reality and the mode of being in a relational way. It will also lead us to acknowledge that human phenomenon will be understood more clearly if we consider how it is related to various contexts.

The Concrete Embodiment of the Intra-Trinitarian Communication

While the essential nature of the triune God remains ineffable and incomprehensible, the concrete historical embodiment of the triune divinity in the ministry of Jesus and the Spirit serves as a foundation upon which we can build a coherent doctrine of the Trinity. God's redemptive participation in the world ultimately consummates the unity of the three divine persons in one being as the eschatological goal of the triune activity. God the Father grounds and unfolds His outreach to the world in the history of redemption. Christ the Son accomplishes the triune economy by capturing and unifying everything under His sovereignty through His death and resurrection. The Holy Spirit continues the redemptive task and empowers the community of believers in the eschatological path to final consummation.

The triune relationship within the divine being embodies the triune economy for the universe. In this manner, the immanent Trinity comes to completion through the economic Trinity. Moltmann asserts,

> The pain of the cross determines the inner life of the triune God from eternity to eternity. If that is true, then the joy of responsive love in glorification through the Spirit determines the inner life of the triune God from eternity to eternity too. Just as the cross of the Son puts its impress on the inner life of the triune God, the history of the Spirit moulds the inner life of the triune God through the joy of liberated creation when it is united with God.[21]

There is a further point in this mutual feature of relationship. The dynamic relationship between the inner lives of God embodies and achieves its goal most vividly in the Trinitarian interaction with our human life. The economic Trinity is not an augmentation of the immanent Trinity, but rather serves as a departure point for leading us to a right understanding of the fully Trinitarian nature of God. As an independent discipline (or a methodological principle) of Christian theology, the economic history of the triune God addresses the general issues and shared themes running through Christian practices.

Thus, the immanence and economy of the Trinity provides us with the critical significance of the historic reality of the Trinitarian theology. This also will assist us in taking into account the context as a focal point of ecological logic.

---

[21] Jürgen Moltmann, *The Trinity and the Kingdom*, trans., Margaret Kohl (San Francisco: Harper and Row, 1981), 161.

Enhancing Relationality in Theology

One issue that stands out, within the recent theological literature, is the concept of relationality. This idea counterbalances the development of the Western individualism in ontology and epistemology which dominated the field since Descartes and his emphasis on the thinking subject. Such individualistic rationalism had an impact of Christian theology, in that it was assumed that God could be described by the use of reason alone. Eberhard Jüngel makes a strong case that the Cartesian understanding of God with its metaphysically grounded certainty has not been capable of disclosing the fullness of the concept of God.[22] This drive for rational certainty of God eclipsed the concrete history of God's encounter with humanity and the creation.

In the twentieth century, the so-called "critical philosophers" have come to the conclusion that the ways in which human beings think and exist are significantly shaped by communal practice and experiences in a network of relations. It is through the historical development of community that people inherit knowledge of what is true and what is useful. The concept of relationality, therefore, has increased in importance within both theology and a wide variety of humanistic disciplines. Personhood is no longer understood as separable or detachable from relationship.

In this sense, the category of relationality is seen as providing a helpful alternative to the purely rationalistic understanding of God's being as well as about human thinking and existence. Both divine and human existence is communally-shaped and relationally-directed. The focus on relationality has also been shaped by various postmodern influences that have urged a rethinking of the concept of personhood. The communitarian nature of God and human beings are increasingly understood as being essential. This mode of thought has been pervasive in a variety of theological disciplines including philosophical theology, moral theology and the like.

However, the way of God's relational existence is something that needs a further corroboration. It has traditionally been the case that Christians understood themselves as "monotheist." Consciously or not, this has led to a belief in a "single divine substance." This picture of an isolated, passionless divinity has obscured God's loving relationship with the world in history. In opposition to this trend, the theological interest in relationality can be ascribed to the achievement of the recent Trinitarian study.[23] It is the triune nature in God which exists relationally. Among theologians, there has been general agreement that Trinitarian virtues mark our own lives because human beings were made in the image of the triune God. However, theologians widely

---

[22]Eberhard Jüngel, *God as the Mystery of the World*, trans. Darrel Guder (Grand Rapids: Eerdmans, 1983), 111.

[23]Cunningham, *These Three Are One: The Practice of Trinitarian Theology* (Malden, MA: Blackwell, 1998), 25.

differ on how the theology of the Trinity should be construed and what this unique doctrine implies for Christian life.

From our experience, we can attest to the fact that we are shaped by virtue of our relations to parents, spouse, and even children. This relational view of human beings shares some commonality with the triune God who exists by virtue of the dynamic relatedness of Father, Son, and Spirit. We live in a so-called "perichoretic universe" in recognition of the triune *perichoresis*. The perichoretic life of the triune God defines and sustains the dynamic relations of the three persons as a unity. The term *perichoresis* "refers to the reciprocal interiority of the Trinitarian persons" in giving and receiving love.[24] The Trinitarian persons are inextricably interdependent and interlinked in their existence and communication. There is no straightforward or hierarchical relationship in the Trinitarian life. Furthermore, the Trinitarian persons empower one another toward completion of redemptive work and toward mutual glorification: For example, God sends His Son into the world (John 13:20); Jesus Christ is glorified and God is glorified in Him (John 13:30); The Holy Spirit makes the Son known and glorified (John 14:26; 16:14); All creation is by and for the Son (Col. 1:16) who reflects the glory of the Father (Heb. 1:3); and, the Spirit reflects the glory of God through the suffering of the church (I Peter 4:14). This perichoretic relationship is also embodied in the life of the church through the indwelling of the Spirit.[25] Gunton suggests that *perichoresis* provides a clue to the integration of the three realms of human activity and thought--such as truth, goodness, and beauty. This is based on a belief that God is the source of all meaning. Truth, goodness, and beauty work together in such a way as to make the message of the gospel more relevant and vivid to human beings.[26] One realm cannot be all-sufficient in undertaking the ministry of the gospel, without referring to the other two, if it is to be Trinitarian. This reciprocal interrelationship indicates the ways in which we interact and communicate with each other as we come to reflect the perichoretic life of the triune God.

Anthropological Significance of the Trinitarian Theology

What does this account of the triune God imply for the practical side of Christian life? This question leads us to consider the impact of the triune divinity upon our understanding of created reality. Gunton argues that the aim of Trinitarian discourse is not to solve our abstract problems about transcendental categories, but to suggest concrete thoughts about the role of human beings in the world by way of engaging such transcendental

---

[24]Miroslav Volf, *After Our Likeness: The Church as the Image of the Trinity* (Grand Rapids: Eerdmans, 1998), 208.
[25]Ibid., 213.
[26]Gunton, 176.

dimensions.[27] Also, Trinitarian life is our life, in that we as Christians are called to share in the very life of God in order to be transformed by the Spirit of God.[28] The Trinitarian inquiry into the ecological structure of human existence will be dealt with first.

Ecological Matrix for Human Beings

There are a plethora of approaches to comprehending religious phenomena. Nevertheless, most approaches to studying religions have focused on the doctrinal integrity of the relevant belief system with a focus on arguments, proof, and reason in undergirding their doctrinal systems.

Contrary to this narrow perspective, ecological thinking attempts to touch upon all aspects of life in an integral way. Religion, from an ecological perspective, is not only concerned with spiritual and moral things (that technology and science cannot deal with), but with material and physical aspects of life as well.[29] Religion informs everyday life and affects its practical realities. Religions are down-to-earth and thus, interconnected with all aspects of human existence. An ecological view of religion asks questions about how religious beliefs affect people's thought and actions, and what their functions might be for individuals in the context of their social and physical existence.[30] The social ecology of religion relates religious beliefs and practices to the social and physical environment of people concerned.

An ecological understanding of religion offers new insight for approaching faith activities. Ecology of religion is deeply concerned with the physical world of religious adherents and its interaction with established beliefs. Thus the complex ways people interact with each other in everyday life can be a field for the ecology of Christian communication. Raynolds and Tanner contend, "What religions do is bound up with the lives of ordinary people, with steering them through the phases of their existence, and not with arguments about"[31] issues that relate to doctrinal controversy.

Religion shapes everyday life. What an ecological approach to religion suggests is that we relate to and explain the force of religious beliefs by reference to the needs of people in everyday strains of their normal life. Raynolds

---

[27]Ibid., 150.
[28]LaCugna, 228.
[29]Vernon Raynolds and Ralph Tanner, *The Social Ecology of Religion* (New York: Oxford University, 1995), 8.
[30]Ibid., 13.
[31]Ibid.

and Tanner, in their ecological studies on religion, define their approach as follows.

> We consider both small-scale and great religions, how they do, wherever they are incorporated into people's live, engage with people in the most matter-of-fact ways, instructing them about their hygiene, their sexual behavior, how when and where to have children, how to manage the difficulties of adolescence, and so on, through the life cycle until death.[32]

Since ecology touches upon the interrelatedness of all aspects of human life, the ecological perspective can be coupled with a Trinitarian discourse which extends itself to the created order. Duane Friesen articulates the relationship of ecological thinking to the doctrine of the Trinity.

> Ecological thinking is integrally connected to what we have said about process. As we learn about the earth and the larger cosmos, we are recognizing more and more that all reality is interconnected and interrelated. Everything that occurs in the universe has an impact on everything else. We belong to a whole. The challenge for modern thought is to transcend the limits of linear, sequential ways of thinking in order to develop a holistic way of thinking that reflects the ecological reality of all being. Thus, we can think today about the Trinity in ways that are reflective of a view of reality as both process and as an ecological whole.[33]

The ecology of the shape of human existence can be drawn from the account of human origins. Moltmann discovers some guiding ideas for an ecological doctrine in the Genesis account. In understanding the human self (as well as gaining the knowledge of God and perceiving the earth), the so-called integrating and integral thinking can serve as a foundation. Assessing the root of the current ecological crisis, Moltmann points out that it is based on the striving of human beings for power and domination. He contends that values and convictions (which prevail in human societies and regulate human life) derive from fundamental human convictions about the meaning and purpose of life. Thus what happens on the personal and relational level of individual human beings cannot be fully understood apart from the larger, diverse systems in which they are located. These systems include natural environments, symbolic systems, cultural tradition, and prevailing belief-systems. The dominion view has not only destroyed the natural environment, but has also deconstructed the interrelatedness between humans and their environment.

In opposition to this human dominion view, the Creation account in Scripture implies that God is essentially relational and communal. Accordingly, the relationship between human beings and other creatures is grounded in their creation by God. Humans and animals share the so-called "solidarity of the

---

[32]Ibid., 25.

[33]Duane Friesen, *Artists, Citizens, Philosophers: Seeking the Peace of the City* (Scottdale, PA: Harold Press, 2000), 94.

sixth day,"³⁴ which means that both human beings and nature are interwoven into the created environment. Human beings are not supposed to dominate the created order, but rather commune and maintain harmony with it.

Moltmann points out, conversely, that the Genesis account provides human beings an opportunity to understand themselves "as a member of the community of creation."³⁵ This awareness calls for a shift in the way humans engage creation. Human life essentially exists "in communication in communion"³⁶ with God, nature, and other human beings, since we are socially interconnected with creation through the creative work of the triune God. Such an ecological foundation underlying the Creation account provides us with some guiding insights for formulating a specifically Christian perception of the being of God and human beings. This ecological attempt at understanding the original shape of human beings will be of significant help in furthering the concept of ecological doctrine as we apply it to other areas such as evangelism and Christian communication.

Sallie McFague, who is deeply concerned with the ecological crisis, contends that ecology, most simply, means "planetary house rules, knowledge of and obedience to the ways of living appropriately in our home, the earth."³⁷ This image comes from an ecological model based on the scientific discovery of "the incredible complexity of the interrelationships and interdependencies among the millions of species of plants and animals on the planet as well as the myriad ways they interact with and depend upon soil, water, chemicals, atmosphere, gases, temperature, and so forth."³⁸ Such awareness of ecology implies that ecology no longer remains a static notion, but rather helps us reformulate the way we treat others and the environment.

The ecological model, thus, leads us to take a multi-dimensional understanding of human existence and behavior. Likewise, Moltmann from the biblical creation asserts that.

> The methods of an ecological doctrine of creation of this kind cannot be one-dimensional. It must use multifarious ways of access to the community of creation, and make people aware of them. We find these approaches in both tradition and experience, in science as well as in wisdom, in intuition but also in deduction. We shall try to look critically at theological traditions in the doctrine of creation. But I should also like to take up new, post-critical scientific methods and ways of thinking. And the approaches of poetic perception and

---

³⁴Ray Anderson, *Spiritual Caregiving as Secular Sacrament: A Practical Theology for Professional Caregivers* (London and New York: Jessica Kingsley, 2003), 66.

³⁵Moltmann, *God in Creation*, 31.

³⁶Ibid., 266.

³⁷Sallie McFague, *The Body of God: An Ecological Theology* (Minneapolis: Fortress, 1993), 5. Here the main point of McFague is to awaken to the reader justice issue and life style in ecological terms. However, still we are able to obtain useful insights from her in order to clarify the implications of ecological framework.

³⁸Ibid., 5-6.

intuition must be integrated as well. The doctrine of creation that emerges will not be one that merely builds up concepts and tries to find definitions, on the philosophical model, important though that is. It will also take up and use symbols, which mould the unconscious mind.[39]

The paragraph above suggests that ecological thinking should not be a linear and analytical enterprise. In ecological terms, the perception of God and creation demands interactive, symbolic, and participatory modes of knowledge. This is especially true when we come to terms with communication and human exchange, since the ecological perception requires us to experientially participate in the whole web as a member of creation.

This ecological perspective has been helpfully employed to articulate the core reality of Christian community and clarify its mission. In defining the nature of the Christian community, the ecological principle concerning the shape of humanity lays a foundation for the ongoing ministry of the Trinity as it unfolds in the work of the Son and the Spirit.

A Trinitarian Understanding of the Human Being

Trinitarian theologians widely agree that human life and the created order are closely bound up with the shape of Trinity. Gunton summarizes, "The human creation, made in the image of God, reflects most directly the divine being in communion."[40] Trinitarian theology does not have to do only with how the divine persons interact with each other, but also how they are revealed in history and what the revelation of the triune divinity implies for human life.

A holistic understanding of the divine image leads to the notion that qualities essential to humanity encompass morality and culture in addition to the cognitive quest for truth. In other words, human being occupies plural dimensions of activity and being. Reformed theologians, such as Barth and Hoekema, generally agree that human representation of God in His image implies that we are made as social beings in covenantal fellowship with God and with others.[41] Such fellowship reflects the original source of the divine relation between Father, Son, and Holy Spirit. Hoekema further suggests that the human qualities in the wake of God's image include a wide range of characteristics including rational power, moral sensitivity, spiritual longing, and aesthetic capacity.[42]

The image of God in the human person mirrors the mode of activity in which the triune God participates. Essential to the biblical view of the image of God is human interaction with God and with others in loving relationship.

---

[39] Moltmann, *God in Creation*, 4.
[40] Gunton, 217.
[41] Anthony Hoekema, *Created in God's Image* (Grand Rapids: Eerdmans, 1986), 50.
[42] Ibid., 70-71.

We are also to take an active role in imaging God by the way we live, namely, by our love for God and for others. The image of God, therefore, is not static but dynamic for Christian life.

The assertion that to be in the image of God is to be in relation with God, other human beings, and the creation, is instructive as we attempt to address the issues that relate to the wholeness of human existence. The important point about the threefold interrelation surrounding the human person is that the proper functioning of the image of God is to be channeled through these three relationships: to God, to neighbor, and to nature. Likewise, knowing God will naturally involve an inter-dynamic relatedness to other human beings and the created order. This idea will assist us in opening up an enhanced way of communicating the Christian truth to those who are spiritually receptive.

The image of God should not be centered upon an inward area (like soul) at the expense of an outward area (like body). The God who takes human flesh confirms that the whole human person, body and soul, is encompassed by the image of God. Incarnation gives the doctrine of the image of God a sense of embodiment. Therefore, human beings are expected to be like God in that they share bodily existence with Jesus. Thus, the carnality of Christian faith can be re-affirmed by way of the image of God informed by the doctrine of Incarnation. This affirmation of embodiment will serve as the important principle upon which we can build implications for Christian communication.

Communicative Significance of Trinitarian Theology

The doctrine of the Trinity brings important points to a variety of theological subjects. The language of God is one such area. The question of how we can speak about God is subsumed under the philosophy of religious language and eventually affects our understanding of Christian communication. If we allow that religion affects the totality of life in an ecological sense and that the human person is to be seen as relational in the biblical accounts, our mode of human communication will be affected by these assumptions. The act of commending the religious faith must, therefore, involves the various elements constituting the whole life.

How then does a revitalized Trinitarian theology of God affect the way in which we communicate with others or we commend the Christian faith to them? This section will seek to re-envision the practice of evangelistic communication in light of a Trinitarian perspective. It will take as its foundational assumptions; 1) communication is at the center of evangelism; and 2) the doctrine of the Trinity involves a specifically Christian way of speaking about

God and summarizes what it means to participate in the communicative life of the triune God through Jesus Christ in the Spirit.

Cunningham, along with LaCugna, insists that the doctrine of the Trinity becomes meaningful only in the context of Christian practices.[43] The relating of a Trinitarian theology to human life in practical ways begins with being attentive to the intra-divine acts. This is because the essential Trinity naturally extends to the realm of the divine economy in human history. It is also because human beings (as part of the created order) are entitled to bear triune marks that echo God's triune nature. To explore the implication of these insights for evangelism (as the ultimate aim of this study), I will attempt to construe the process of human communication in the light of the Trinitarian virtues and features.

Relational Persuasion

Language does not contain any significant properties in itself, but produces meaning and effect in engagement with relationships. Meaning is formed and delivered by the way of process of relationships among rhetorical subjects and objects. In order for persuasive communication to occur, there must be a dynamic interaction of those who are included in the process of communication. Persuasion results from a variety of interdependent relationships among the rhetor, audience, and argument.[44] In fact, meaning is made and understood through the formation of relationships among a variety of factors: speaker, audience, message, and media.

This is why the process of communication cannot be fully understood from an atomistic and individualistic perspective. Communication requires each other and cannot exist in isolation from one another. Persuasion does not always take place in a temporal, linear, and logical sequence, but rather in context where speaker and listener interact mutually.

The Trinitarian way of existence is a representative form of the relational context in which human beings and the created order are grounded. The triune God engages with the created order in a relational and cooperative way. Redemptive history itself can be best understood in the wake of the Trinitarian economy. Thus, the mode of relating in context is crucial to communicating and understanding any given meaning. In this respect, looking at the Trinity as a model of how God carries out his mission provides helpful insights for relational communication.

The essential role of relationality needs to be highlighted as we come to terms with Trinitarian thought. When we envision the Christian person, we tend to think in terms of individual persons of God involved in accidental relations from which they can extricate themselves at will. Similarly, the Trinity was often misunderstood as three individual and sequential manifestations

---

[43]LaCugna, 4.
[44]Cunningham, 116.

of the one God according to various ages. The triune God, however, is better expressed and understood as involving a dynamic participation with each other.

The way in which the triune God exists in Three persons should not be conceived of as individuals who happen to have come into relation with one another, but rather as a reality that is so mutually self-participative that distinctions can no longer be drawn. The modern era has tempted us to think of ourselves as autonomous individuals; but upon deeper reflection, we recognize that such absolute distinction fail to describe the communion and mutual participation we seek to embody.[45]

Relational context is the ground on which persuasive communication occurs by underscoring mutual participation. Effective communication is characterized by "the ability to move outside oneself, to become 'other' to oneself, so that one hears the speech from the other's point of view, and not merely from one's own."[46] This relational interaction is apparent in the immanent and economic mission of the triune God. The most representative act of the triune God is self-communication, or self-producing as described in the Nicene Creed. God the Father had begotten Jesus the Son, and Jesus had breathed the Spirit upon those who believe in Him.

The redemptive economy of the triune God is fundamentally grounded in the internal self-differentiation of God. In addition, God's self-differentiation extends also into the realm of the created world. God produces the world through creation and even becomes flesh in the body of Jesus. Irenaeus asserts that the triune mission serves as the foundation for creation and redemption by God's two hands: "the incarnation of the Word in Christ" and "the pouring out of the Spirit upon the church." What is fundamental for divine activity in the triune mode is an act of producing among the three persons of God. The triune God is self-producing and at the same time self-differentiating. The one and the three exist without subsuming of one into the other.

Since individuals are not defined in the abstract but in the context, the character of persons becomes apparent only through relating to others. God's self-differentiation becomes basic to God's self-producing: producing God (Father, Son and Spirit) as well as the world. As God self-differentiates within His triune nature, He differentiates the world. "From the Christian perspective, the world is not created out of God; it is created out of nothing (*ex nihilo*). God and creation are thus separated by . . . an 'infinite qualitative difference.'"[47] In spite of the essential chasm between God and the world, this differentiation does not imply eternal distance. The biblical accounts clearly point to the knowledge of God given to us in the Incarnation of the Word and interpreted to us through the pouring out of the Spirit. This is how God produces the world as well as produces God Himself. One important point we

---

[45]Cunningham, 169.
[46]Ibid., 110.
[47]Ibid., 74-75.

can take from productive triune activities is that God communicates in relations. God carries out His creative and redemptive missions in cooperation with the Son and the Spirit.

As stated earlier, persuasion results from the interdependent relationship. Interestingly, a rhetorical construction can be applied to the dynamic triune relationship in which the three persons exist with one another, giving to and receiving from one another. Cunningham presents the following application of a rhetorical construction to the Trinitarian relationship.

> The relationship among the rhetor, audience, and argument mirrors that among Source (the Father), Wellspring (the Son), and the Living Water (the Spirit): the rhetor becomes a rhetor only when producing an argument for an audience; the argument becomes argument when so produced; the (constructed) audience becomes audience upon being postulated as the target of the argument by the rhetor. Certainly, the human being who is about to take on the role of rhetor pre-exists the rhetorical context; but that person cannot be named by a relational term such as rhetor until the other elements of the process if rhetorical invention are also in place. Only then do the relations of "speaking" and "constructing" play a role. Similarly a group of people assembled in a room, waiting, is not yet an "audience" in any strong sense; and even when they do hear the argument, they are not its "original" audience, for an audience first had to be constructed in the mind of the rhetor in order for argument to be formed. Each of the three causes the others and is simultaneously caused by the others; there are no logical, temporal, or causal hierarchies among them. And just the same goes for the Trinity; the Three implicate one another, making one another what they are.[48]

In other words, the meaning-generation out of rhetorical process (or effective communication) depends on the inter-dynamic relation of participants and media. The way the triune God produces and communicates is in accordance with this inter-relational model. The three unique activities are incorporated into one in order to deliver a redemptive meaning. It can be inferred from the above discussion that God reveals His saving love and message to the world in relational acts in much the same way as He exists as relation in producing essence onto the world.

In the process of communicating the Christian truth, this relational character of communication assists us in looking beyond linear transmissions of the given message to the various settings that condition communication. The triune God engages with human beings relationally as Father, the Son, and the Spirit for the purpose of carrying out a redemptive mission.

John Milbank distances Christian theology from the realm of formal logic by claiming that the divine nature of relationality and process takes precedence over fixed essence or substance.[49] Milbank asserts that Christian theol-

---

[48]Ibid., 114.

[49]John Milbank, "'Postmodern Critical Augustinianism': A Short *Summa* in Forty Two Responses to Unasked Questions," *Modern Theology* 7, no. 3 (April 1991): 225-37.

ogy has been construed to hold the concept of fixed essence in articulating a concept of human beings and God. The doctrine of the Trinity is an affirmation that God is Himself community and highlights the relational ontology of theology proper. In contrast to dogmatic and abstract speculation, this practical and relational approach to the Trinity can help elucidate the Gospel and the way it is communicated. The essence of the divine existence and mission is relational and, in turn, necessitates a diversity of engaging with the world in order to communicate who God is and what His purpose is all about. Thus, an acknowledgement of God's relational way of communication will point to the need for the multiple modes of communication that are inferred from Trinitarian virtues.

Plurality of Communication

According to Cunningham, the way in which the relational God acts (whether in intra- or inter-relation) parallels the way a musical symphony is expressed through various instruments. In music, multiple themes and notes are not necessarily contrastive or disruptive. Also, it is never a zero-sum game with one prominent note overwhelming the others. This musical analogy is developed by Cunningham to account for the diversity of Trinitarian acts of communication. The so-called "polyphony" (poly=many, phony=sound) explains the harmony which can ensue from a combination of different tones and notes. Cunningham claims, "The category of polyphony provides us with a critical perspective from which to examine all competing claims about God and the world."[50] A Trinitarian polyphony functions as a corrective to the purely conceptual and rationalistic portrait of Jesus and the Gospel. Communicating the Christian gospel is not best accomplished by way of a single system of truth based on universal reason or logic, which tells us what reality is like. Rather, the gospel is better communicated by a polyphonic process. This is how the triune God acts and His revelation involves the whole created order. Without being limited to formal structures of logic, the polyphonic approach encourages us to include all aspects of culture, multiple senses, and the created order in sketching out and experiencing the triune God. This approach also recognizes that "the entire shape of the Christian life (even aesthetics in addition to metaphysics and ethics[51]) is a more powerful argument than the most carefully constructed syllogism."[52] Gunton asserts that the Trinitarian God "contains within himself a form of plurality in relation and creates a world which reflects the richness of his being" and enables us "better to conceive something of the unity in variety of human culture."[53]

---

[50] Cunningham, 129.
[51] Colin Gunton refers to those three as the representative focuses of human activity throughout his book. See Gunton, *The One and The Many*, 176.
[52] Cunningham, 310.
[53] Gunton, *The One and the Many*, 177.

The polyphonic beauty of Christian life that mirrors harmonious Trinitarian cooperation is best located in the practice of the local church. The local church is responsible for administering sacraments, preaching the Word, and pastoral care. Communication scholars claim that, in terms of communicating process, high ritual or performance is the most prominent reflection of the plural combination of arts.[54] Most rituals necessarily require the participants to experience a variety of human senses: visual, oral, aural, olfactory, and tactile. This communicative insight rings true with one of the features addressed by Trinitarian discourse, in that the mission of the Trinity runs parallel to the polyphony of music.

Through Jesus' baptism and the Eucharist the three persons of the Trinity participate together. Jesus' baptism is obviously a Trinitarian event in which the Father spoke, the Spirit hovered above like a dove, and Jesus immersed himself into the water. The Trinitarian presence is invoked at the moment in the Eucharist as well. The Eucharist can help us come into contact with God in an immediate way as well as acknowledge the ongoing reality of God's participation in our lives through Christ's body and blood.[55] Participating in the body of the Son invokes the real presence of the Trinity who self-communicates as well as brings us into communion with each other. The Eucharist also makes use of a variety of senses: seeing, listening, bread-breaking, and wine-drinking, and so on. Thus we can conclude that the way the triune God communicates His presence and engages human being involve a plurality of communicative channels, for the whole created order bears His creative marks.

Incarnational Qualities: Intelligibility and Materiality

In redemptive history, the economy of triune God has been revealed most clearly in the saving love and providential plan of the incarnate Son and has been carried out by the continuing work of the Holy Spirit. When we assert that God is relationally engaged with humanity, our focus is on the overlap between God and humanity. Also, the redemptive story is narrated through God's triune intimate mutual participation in the created realm. God's participation in human history became most evident in the Incarnation of the Son.

In this scheme, the main focus will be on the Incarnation. The Incarnational event provides Christianity with the clearest manifestation of the link between God and humanity. As was mentioned earlier, Trinitarian discourse can begin only with an economic presentation of the triune God in history. At the peak of the economic Trinity in history and in the world is the God-human Jesus Christ. In the created order, Jesus Christ stands out at the heart of the Trinity.

---

[54]Ruth Finnegan, *Communicating: The Multiple Modes of Human Interconnection* (London & New York: Routledge, 2002), 238. Finnegan sees this mix of art at the highest expression of communication.

[55]Cunningham, 173.

Incarnation permeates all of Jesus' actions throughout his earthly ministry including teaching, healing, signs and wonders, and suffering and death. The mission of Jesus does not encompass all of the Trinitarian communication with the world, but rather the focal point of the economic Trinity is made manifest in the person of Christ. Cunningham makes the point that the most definite form of the divine revelation came "not as a statement, nor as a set of propositions, but as a human being."[56] If God embodied Himself in history through the person of Jesus Christ, then speaking of God is not just a matter of words, but also of images, and bodily actions.

It should be noted, therefore, that "in the economic self-communication the intra-Trinitarian self-communication is present in the world in a new way, namely, under the veil of historical words, signs and actions, and ultimately in the figure of the man Jesus of Nazareth."[57] Thus, the Incarnation must be seen as God's way of communicating, a way which identifies with those who seek mutual understanding and reconciliation.

The biblical narratives concerning Jesus report that the incarnate God went through multiple human experiences. In human form, he was born, raised, tried, stripped, mocked, and crucified by human beings. God's polyphonic and relational character is best demonstrated in the event of Jesus' baptism. In that single event, the three persons of the triune God engaged together. The Incarnation, therefore, involves the triune transcendent God taking on all aspects of humanity from pregnancy and birth to death and beyond.

The two main points which come to light in Incarnational communication are the intelligibility and materiality of Christian truth. An over-emphasis on the transcendent uniqueness of the Trinity engenders a negative theology, which claims that human language cannot contain the expression of God. This position is called "apophasis" (denial of speech), and holds that God is beyond all categories of human thought and words. Thus, the human person can describe God only through negative expressions such as "God is not good," (because God's character cannot be defined within human conceptions of goodness) or through silence.

LaCugna offers a more helpful engagement with this apophatic way of theological discourse. She comments that negative discourse about God "leads not into absence or nothingness but into the presence of the God who surpasses thoughts and words and even the desire for God. . . . Apophasis requires letting go of every controlling concept or image for God so that the living God may enlighten the darkness of our minds."[58] LaCugna sees the possibility of articulating the depth of the triune faith in the midst of "Christian community," or "by analogy."[59] This viewpoint is based on the notion that the God-relationship may surpass the grasp of objective conceptual categories.

---

[56] Ibid., 83.
[57] LaCugna, 220.
[58] Ibid., 326.
[59] Ibid., 330.

Truth can be, therefore, encountered by way of communal practice and narrative or analogies. While partially agreeing with these two methodologies for positive discourse about God, I propose that we also rethink the Incarnation as the focal point in which human beings come into contact with the triune God in an intelligible way.

James Smith presents an Incarnational account of language as a third way for to speak something intelligible beyond conceptual expression. Smith suggests that all the world is an "icon" and so also are words.[60] In other words, all things can function as a sign for the communication of meaning. This suggestion is, in fact, congruous with the earlier statement that the whole created order reflects the triune God. Smith, therefore, endeavors to represent the category of language in a broader sense. Then, he goes on to say that the Incarnation is an immanent sign of the transcendent God appearing in the flesh.[61] He also asserts, "God's Incarnational appearance is precisely a condescension to the conditions of finite, created perceivers. How does he appear otherwise? The Incarnation signals a connection with transcendence...."[62]

It must also be noted that revelation itself preconditions the recipients because the message of an argument necessitates an audience. If any given message cannot be communicated to an audience, what role does the argument play? The revelation process comes to nothing unless it is made comprehensible to its recipients. Conversely, the Trinitarian participation in human history adumbrates the possibility that the divine message was expressed in human language. The Incarnation of the Son was the peak of this communicative event.

Incarnation reopens the way to intelligibility in Christian communication. The doctrine of the Incarnation gives a new insight as to how we can speak of God. In order to have a right understanding of the Incarnation, we need to attempt to get beyond the word-centered approach to the Logos. Along with this idea, it should be remembered that the Incarnation allowed the possibility of speaking of God in broadly human terms.

Summary

My central concern in this paper is to show how a theological reflection on the Trinity can provide a comprehensive view of Christian anthropology and communication. An inquiry into the nature of the triune God enables us to grasp the dynamic interrelatedness of God to Father, Son, and Spirit, which is also reflected historically in the consummation which involves creating and renewing the universe. Human beings are made in the image of God whose inner life is by virtue of *perichoresis*, which self-produces and self-

---

[60]James Smith, *Speech and Theology: Language and the Logic of Incarnation* (New York: Routledge, 2002), 117.
[61]Ibid., 123.
[62]Ibid., 126.

communicates between the Persons. This divine origin of human life enables us to understand our distinctive manner of existence in interrelated dynamics with the creation and recognize a wide range of activities and relations in human interconnections. As the triune God embodies Himself in the world through the unfolding of His redemptive economy, we are entitled to take into account the whole domains of life as we communicate with others. This is the ecological ground for human communication. This profound quality of the triune God should be reflected in the Christian community and its witness. As LaCugna suggests, the Christian community is to be "the icon of the Trinity where there is sheer joy in mutual love, the fullest possible exchange and interdependence among persons."[63]

The Trinitarian pattern of thought helps us get beyond a mathematical and mechanical way of communication and to look to relational and aesthetic communication as essential to opening up the possibility of intelligible discourse about God. Linear or logical modes of communication, based on rationalism (which had prevailed in the modern era), were once employed as the main means for evangelism. The doctrine of the Trinity, however, should not be communicated in such a manner to promote a simplistic discourse of God. In addition, the mode of interaction between the Father, the Son, and the Spirit reflects a more profound interaction in a polyphonic and relational way.

This is a compelling line of argument, if we accept the fact that, all relations cannot be described in a linear, objective, but rather reflect an organic, pluralistic pattern. However, much of our difficulties with evangelistic communication stem from a mechanical and technocratic view, which fails to see the interrelatedness of the world and human relations. Such a mechanistic worldview digresses from the Trinitarian framework of nature and things. On the other hand Trinitarian theology offers a worldview to deal with what is wrong with our thought and behavior in the world.

---

[63]Catherine M. LaCugna, "Freeing the Christian Imagination," *Dialog* 33, no. 3 (Summer 1994), 194.

Chapter Two

Descriptive Phase: Mechanistic Domination of Communication and Evangelism

Having established the theological paradigm for the interrelated, ecological thinking approach to evangelistic communication, this chapter now turns to the assessment of practical problems that relate to communication and evangelism. Additionally, the theological worldview addresses the problem of the human condition. The present chapter, therefore, attempts to describe how from a Trinitarian perspective, the manners in which we approach evangelistic communication are affected by a different vision of reality.

According to Fritjof Capra (a proponent of the New Science movement), there are two worldviews that are in a sharp conflict: mechanistic and ecological.[64] Each worldview has its own system of interpretation about the world and humanity and spawns a particular pattern of common practice. The mechanistic world view has engendered technological culture, which greatly influences the practice of evangelistic communication. Before delving into the technological influences over evangelistic communication, this chapter explores the more fundamental thought-frame underlying technological culture. As compared to the Trinitarian vision of human existence and communication which offers an integrated and ecological view, the mechanistic worldview offers a disconnected and dualistic vision of human life and nature.

The Underlying Worldview of the Technological Culture

In order to deal with the ideological aspect of the technological culture, this study will take a brief glimpse of how Western thinking has arrived at such principles in understanding nature and life and how they have generated the

---

[64]Fritjof Capra, *The Turning Point: Science, Society, and the Rising Culture* (New York: Bantam, 1982), 16.

mechanistic, transmission view of communication by disconnecting body and soul, subject and object, and content and context.

The Western Mechanistic Worldview

Greek philosophy understood human beings as rational animals, which has led to reason being regarded as the distinct mark of human essence. Plato emphasized that sense experience yields only fallible opinion, not authentic knowledge, for the material world is in perpetual flux, and easily deceives.[65] The latter is always considered to be the authentic authority for truth, and the former is seen as illusion. This dualistic perception of material and mental or spiritual realms laid the foundation for the mechanistic worldview.

Greek dualism had a tremendous influence on the development of Western philosophy at the same time that the church was shaping its own identity. According to platonic thought, the spiritual realm is considered superior to the material. Greek dualism tended to be less amenable towards cultural manifestations (such as the visual arts and images in churches) but rather pursued a metaphysical approach that separated the subject from the object. With regard to specific cultural forms, Christian churches in the platonic tradition have largely neglected the role of images in Christian worship and life, while the Eastern Orthodox churches have used the images in positive ways. Moreover, the *Logos* in the Gospel of John, chapter one was often understood to be equivalent to Plato's ideal form and was employed for building an apologetic case toward the Greeks. Many Christian doctrines were translated and reformulated according to this platonic idea. It follows from this tradition that the Logos had been considered to be equal to the concept of Christian truth within the content of evangelism.

Modern Dualism

While the disengagement of content from context in communication has largely been based on the physical/spiritual dichotomy of ancient Greek philosophy, the emergence of the fully blown mechanistic worldview began with Descartes. Repudiating the Aristotelian doctrine of the innate teleological movement of an individual, Descartes presented the whole material world as a mechanical system, which runs according to abstract principles and which can be mathematically measured.[66]

In addition, this mechanistic worldview has been closely associated with the theistic tradition of the West, in which God is understood as a kind of engineer. The world is a machine, and God is the Mover of the world. The Chris-

---

[65]Wright, "Platonism" in *New Dictionary of Theology*, eds. Sinclair B. Ferguson, David F. Wright and James I. Packer (Downers Grove, IL: InterVarsity Press, 1988), 518.

[66]Frederick Copleston, *A History of Philosophy*, Vol. IV (New York: Image Books, 1994),, 138.

tian understanding of God has been shaped by this mechanistic worldview in developing the notion that God is the ultimate Mover of extended entities. Both mind and matter are creations of God, "who represented their common point of reference, being the source of the exact natural order and of the light of reason that enabled the human mind to recognize this order."[67] The world and things are grasped as objects to be moved and controlled by human reason as the rational subject. Foundational to the mechanistic worldview is the human ability to think and reason. In this way, the dichotomy between object and subject had remained until the modern period.

The notion of the world as object (extended bodies) gave rise to the object-centered approach in addressing the substance of the world. An object-centered approach can be applied to culture and art, which function as the media for communication. The object-centered understanding of cultural works is rooted in this mechanistic dualism of Western worldview. Within the Western intellectual tradition, material and sensual realms are treated as objects to be rationally analyzed and henceforth treated pejoratively.

This stance toward art exemplifies the object-centered approach, which means that when relating to a particular media, people tend to separate themselves from the communicate realm of media rather than participate in it. Object-centered thought excludes the subject that is before and in the given media, and only seeks detached and alienated speculation.

The traditional Western view of the human person and nature has developed under the influence of the mechanistic paradigm. It prioritizes soul or mental activity over body or material, and treats the world as extensions that can be controlled and exploited by the human mind. Also, it had led to the notion that the object in human culutral activity is separable from the life of the human subject. The relation between human being, and the creation, therefore, is defined by controllable and manageable mechanistic terms. This dichotomized and mechanistic thought-frame sets the stage for us to review the technological culture it has produced today.

Summary

I have briefly sketched the historical development of the mechanistic worldview to show how this underlying thinking departs from a Trinitarian view of nature and human beings. While the Trinitarian structure clearly emphasizes the relational and interconnected nature of creation, the mechanistic worldview has led to a disconnected notion of soul and body, nature and humanity, and object and subject throughout history. I do not mean to suggest, however, that the whole thinking paradigm throughout history has been tainted by such mechanistic thinking. Rather this study focuses on major sources that have influenced the present technological culture that, in turn, impacts the practice of evangelistic communication.

---

[67]Capra, 60.

This thought-frame leads to a more monolithic approach to communication and evangelism in a technological culture whereas the present chapter asserts that the manner in which we communicate the gospel has been largely tainted by the technological cultural form. This leads us back to the immediate setting that induces the mechanistic application of evangelistic programs as was set forth in the Introduction.

Modern Technological Culture and Its Impact upon Communication

The development of science and technology changes the environment in which we live and then affects the way in which we approach reality. In the ensuing discussion, this study attemtps to describe how such a mechanistic view of value effects the ways in which we do communication and evangelism. Also, it seeks to demonstrate that technological culture plays a central role in making communication fragmented, overly efficient, standardized, and linear--all of which which leads to a distorted and limited view of evangelism.

It must be noted beforehand that technology itself is not only treated pejoratively in this study, although I frequently maintain a critical perspective. Technology can open up new levels of human interconnection. Digital technology, for example, makes possible human experience in communication to be more interactive than in the past. It also can encourage us to engage more in audiovisual realities. Compared to media technologies in the previouse age, these new qualities of the digital technology shape the persons who are more inclined to affection and experience. This development should have a significant impact on our understanding of Christian ministry.[68] There are challenges and opportunities that each technological development constitutes.

However, the word "technology" is not used here to mean new scientific skill or development, but rather a social and cultural form which has arisen from the development of science and the mechanistic worldview. To clarify, when I refer to "technological culture, system, or society," or "technique," I mean the social environment we live in. By "mechanistic worldview," I mean the underlying conception, historically developed, that has engendered such a social and cultural form. Here the technological culture means a social form that is dominated by mechanistic thiking.[69]

---

[68]Pierre Babin with Mercedes Iannone, *The New Era in Religious Communication* (Minneapolis: Fortress, 1991), 17.

[69]It is Jacques Ellul who first raised concerns within Christian circles, about the threats and crises that the technological society would bring to humanity. To Ellul, it is "technique" that defines modern society and advocates the entire remaking of life not as a machine, but as a mindset. See Jacques Ellul, *The Technological Society: A Penetrating Analysis of Our Technical Civilization and of the Effect of an Increasingly Standardized Culture on the Future of Man* (New York: Vintage Books, 1964), 142.

Technological development gives rise to particular values and attitudes which effect all of human life rather than just improving a certain area of human life. It has been influential in forming the concrete practices of human society. If we define culture as a collective form of "social behaviors as their ordering principle, the meaning dimension of social life, a force directing action, and an action-governing mechanism,"[70] we can see that the technological system has arisen within "culture" as one of the dominant forces which organize modern society. The area of communication is also affected by this cultural force.

The development of each communication technology changed the way people thought as well as the way they exchanged information and knowledge. The invention of writing itself in the ancient times was crucially important to changing the way people approached knowledge at that point of history. Printing technology made a notable difference in the way in which human senses were used. Oral culture was not defined by its logical precision, whereas writing culture placed more emphasis on clarity and logical consistency. As Walter Ong rightly puts it,

> The distancing which writing effects develops a new kind of precision in verbalization by removing it from the rich but chaotic existential context of much oral utterance....Orally managed languagge and thought is not noted for analytic precision....Of course, all language and thought is to some degree analytic....But written words sharpen analysis, for the individual words are called on to do more. To make yourself clear without gesture, without facial expression, without intonation, without a real hearer, you have to foresee circumspectly all possible meanings a statement may have for any possible reader in any possible situation, and you have to make your language work so as to come clear all by itself.[71]

Writing is, in fact, a solitary activity while orality stresses cooperate sense of learning and social responsibility. This individual character of writing leads to an emphasis on introspection and self-examination, whereas "the original, genetically programmed form of human communication is two-way: We both hear and speak."[72] In much the same vein, the invention of printing press brings the isolated and individualized culture of writing to a different level. Books preceded printing. However, the extent to which printing transformed the existing literary culture was remarkable. Spelling became uniform, punctuation followed standarized rules, and alphabetical order was widely used.[73] The invention and spread of printing, therefore, led to promo-

---

[70] Kathryn Tanner, *Theories of Culture: A New Agenda for Theology* (Minneapolis: Fortress, 1997), 37-38.

[71] Walter Ong, *Orality and Literacy: The Technologizing of the Word* (New York: Methuen, 1982), 104.

[72] Mitchell Stephens, *The Rise of the Image the Fall of the Word* (New York: Oxford University Press, 1998), 165.

[73] Ibid., 29.

tion of the precise, analytical and linear thnking,[74] which serves as the foundation for modern way of communication.

Since human life is essentially social and thus shaped in relation to communicative interactions, communication is fundamental to human life and involves every mode of human existence.[75] Every form of living and social systems has a communicative dimension. Nevertheless, there have been cases in which communication is reduced to a matter of technique or language which bears the marks of technological culture in combination with the Enlightenment exaltation of thought or reason above "other modes of communication."[76]

In addition, the mechanistic and monologic understanding of com-munication has, to some degree, evolved with the development of the technological system in general. While communication technologies were originally designed as instruments to get the message across, the cultural traits of technopoly have come to infiltrate the the modes of communication as a complete expression of human existence. As technological invention has progressed, the principles underneath it such as objectivity, efficiency, standarization, and measurement permeated the whole of human life including communication.[77] In what follows, this study will depict the features of such technologically shaped communication practices in more detail.

Communication Practices Shaped by Technological Culture

In contemporary society, technique or technological culture[78] (whatever it is labeled) becomes a more important driving force of social development than the ends it is supposed to serve. Technique became an end in itself and the society is organized around its mandate. Thus technique, as an ideology of the technological society, needs to be discussed with reference to the capacity of human reasoning and judgment.

---

[74]Ibid., 208f. Stephens here argues that the formative influence of printing technology was far diverse than we expect. "Print's linear, one-word-follows-another, one-thing-at-a-time logic is perhaps its greatest strength. Expanding on the work begun by writing in the time of the pre-Socratic philosopher Heraclitus, print has pulled us in an exceedingly profitable direction. We owe it much: modern science, modern medicine, modern democracy, our reformations and enlightenments-all were advanced by the printed word." Even he includes the governing structure as being operated by the logic of printing culture.

[75]Stephen K. Pickard, *Liberating Evangelism: Gospel Theology and the Dynamics of Communication* (Harrisburg, PA: Trinity Press International, 1999), 19.

[76]Ibid., 20.

[77]Postman, 42.

[78]In the discussion that follows, such vocabularies as "technique," "technological mindset," "*techne*," and technicism that describe the way of thinking in which the technological culture governs will be interchangeably used in order to avoid repetition.

More specifically, in this sense, Aristotle differentiates three modes of human rationality:[79] *theoria* (contemplative reasoning), *phronesis* (practical reasoning), and *techne* (productive reasoning). While contemplative reasoning has to do with the purely theoretical dimension of human thinking, practical reasoning has to do with human action in the social sphere. On the same practical level, productive reasoning emerges when human rationality focuses on effect and product as its utmost concern. Brad Kallenberg notes four distinctive marks of *techne*, the so-called "productive reasoning" or technological reasoning, as follows.

First, *techne* procedes without requiring the internal relation of agent to the actions or the products in question, while practical reasoning accords significance to the human role and relations. Technological development, in other words, needs no reference to contextual and relational factors. Kallenberg illustrates this with manufacturing process of shoes.

> Shoes, for example, are complete in themselves and are ontologically distinct from the cobbler. In contrast, the ends of praxis cannot be distinguished from the doing of it or from the doer of it. For example, when I respond to my neighbor in a particular manner, say, that of kindness, this pattern of action is itself the goal of my acting in this manner. Furthermore, I as an agent have more at stake in practicing kindness than has the cobbler in shoes since my action (party) is constitutive of my own character, whereas for cobbler, they're just shoes.[80]

In a world where a technological culture governs, the end is not necessarily connected with or engage in the process or context on which the process of production must be based.

Secondly, Kallenberg maintains that *techne* only needs "bare knowledge,"[81] while practical reasoning requires numerous "on-the-spot judgments"[82] in different situations. The technological mindset, therefore, tends to rely on predeterminded knowledge and information. Kallenberg recalls Aristotle's saying, "to do this to the right person, to the right extent, at the right time, with the right aim, and in the right way, that is not for everyone, nor is it easy."[83] Aristotle rightly understands that while the technological mindset pursues preconditioned and mechanical information for action, goals, manners, and processes for every action tend to vary with each new situation.

Third (and as a consequence of the second), Kallenberg argues that "*techne* has to do with univeralizing rules for procedures which govern production."[84]

---

[79]Brad Kallenberg, *Ethics as Grammar: Changing the Postmodern Subject* (Notre Dame, IN: University of Notre Dame Press, 2001), 162. Much of discussion about characteristics of *techne* as productive reasoning will follow from Kallenberg's book.
[80]Ibid., 162.
[81]Ibid.
[82]Ibid., 163.
[83]Ibid.
[84]Ibid.

The technological mindset tends to generalize the rules for action and set them forth as applicable to every situation regardless of difference in time and space while overlooking particularity.

Fourth, *techne* tends to hold to the linear conception that the application of general and universal rules is straighforward and sufficient, while Aristotle upholds that "a universal does contain its own application."[85] There is an assumption inherent in the technologically oriented mind that rules or principles formed out of a given context can be directly and inductively applicable to different situations. Such a linear and logical syllogism runs the risk of overlooking particulars, which are crucial to planning and implementing actions.

For now, understanding certain features basic to a technological worldview will be helpful for gaining insights into the technological system and its influence upon the ways in which we communicate and attempt to persuade. Given those four characteristics of technological culture drawn from Aristotle's assessment of productive reasoning--or *techne*--the next section will be devoted to a further articulation of those features in regard to modern technological culture and its critical effect on how we communicate.

The Fragmentation of Communication

Modern technology combined with the Enlightenment worldview is predisposed to focus on a certain area of human action without taking into account the fact that many aspects of human life are intertwined like a web. Thus, it has caused human society to disconnect the social forms that constitute human life. With regards to knowledge and communication, contemporary society holds that a mere fact exists for itself and is able to retain significance without reference to related factors.

In this milieu of technological rationalism, the neccesary interconnectedness between knowledge and context, as well as between rational activity and human purpose is rejected. The mentality of a technological society drives itself towards autonomous and fragmented rationality.

In many situations, however, such a narrow perspective is limiting. For instance, human communication requires some intimacy. Effective speakers should know the concerns and interests of a specific audience to whom they are going to relate. In the past, face to face relationship laid the foundation which made communication possible. However, with the development of information technology, transmission of the message tends to depend more on communication through technological media such as computer modem, fax machine, visual images, and so on. The communication scholar Quentin J. Schultze issus an warning about the over-dependence on seductively "useful"

---

[85]Ibid.

informtation technology, because it is likely to deprive us of intimate contacts in communicative interaction.

> The more time and evergy we spend using information technologies, the less likely we are to know intimately the world around us. Information technologies foster secondhand knowledge about rather than more intimate knowledge of. Informationism produces . . . a kind of knowing disengaged from the deeper drama of life.[86]

Fragmentation is, thus, the salient phenomenon that technological society brings to life. Now, communication in an information age can seemingly exist and function by itself without reference to human relationship and free of context. The disconnection of human communication from relational context is further intensified by the commodification of knowledge and information. Once any message is disengaged from a living context, it runs the risk of being reduced to a commodity. Information as commodity is transient without consideration for the context out of which the message makes its meaning fully understood.

The threat to human communication in light of its commodification is also created by technological advancement that attempts to govern all forms of cultural life. This aspect is further elaborated by Albert Borgmann's concept of "device paradigm." Borgmann argues that technological progress brings better tools which improve human society at the surface level and remove burdens from our life. This might appear to bring hope and liberation, but it robs humanity of opportunities to participate in the long standing construction of human community.

Borgmann further explains this critical drift by distinguishing between things and devices. "A thing . . . is inseparable from its context, namely its worlds, and from our commerce with the thing and its world, namely, engagement."[87] Objects, in the world, which human beings engage through physical, mental, or social participation he refers to as things. Engaging with a thing, thus, involves other aspects of human senses, and cannot be seperated from context and relationship.

For example, Borgmann exemplifies the fireplace or stove as things by noting how, engagement with them, helps build up human relationships and encourages interaction with other aspects of human life. A fireplace (like a hearth in the past) is a focus that gathers family members and allows them an "experience of the world through the manifold sensibility of the body" through physical engagement and learning how to operate it.[88]

---

[86]Quentin J. Schultze, *Habits of the High-Tech Heart: Living Virtuously in the Information Age* (Grand Rapids: Baker, 2002), 32.

[87]Albert Borgmann, *Technology and the Character of Contemporary Life: A Philosophical Inquiry* (Chicago: The University of Chicago Press, 1984), 41.

[88]Ibid., 41-42.

With the advent of the automatic heating system, however, the function of fireplace came to be seen solely as one of providing warmth which resulted in the loss of interconnected social and generational relationship building as was extant in the pretechnological setting. On the other hand, the central heating plant emerged as a device providing efficiency by removing burdens such carrying wood and watching the fire. In spite of this benefit, Borgmann notes that such a device plays a critical role in disconnecting people from bodily and social connection.

> A device such as a central heating plant procures mere warmth and disburdens us of all other elements. These are taken over by the machinery of the device. The machinery makes no demands on our skill, strength, or attention, and it is less demanding the less it makes its presence felt.[89]

It cannot be discounted that the device offers great benefits. The promise of the technological device was to liberate people by conquering the scourges of humanity and enrich human life. Nevertheless, it should be noted that this disburdening has also come to disengage people from contact with things and deprives humans of an opportunity to enhance social relationships. While the device provides social disburdenment, it exacts a cost of social anonymity at the expense of relational development.[90] The most significant result of this transormation to a device is that a thing becomes a commodity enarmored with convenience and efficiency, which stands free from human engagement in context.

Being combined with the anonymous role of machinery, such commodification takes the form of a device paradgim. Once the device paradigm is interwoven into the fabric of our family and society, we come to have far fewer tasks in which we can participate together. For example, over-emphasis on communication devices such as advertising pamphlets and radio broadcasting do not leave any room for interaction of knowledge and information grounded in a relational world. In other words, technology has taken over many of the relational and communal tasks. What needs to be challenged is not technology per se, but the fact that the device paradigm has become the primary pattern by which much of our society operates.

The Pursuit of Efficient Communication

Technological rationalism, according to Ellul, serves a single purpose: "efficiency"[91] which is the foremost value the technological system enforces upon human life. The fate of the technological society hinges upon the expectation of greater efficiency. The utmost goal of technological rationalism becomes obvious. Under the auspices of objective rationalism, technological

---

[89] Ibid., 42.
[90] Ibid., 44.
[91] Ellul, *The Technological Society*, 21.

society aims at gaining efficiency which must be maintained at all costs and at every level of human life.

With the multiplication and reduction of means, reason engages in selecting the most efficient technique for the maximum result. Repeatedly, technique emerging from this rationalistic quest imposes the universal value of efficiency upon human life. Ellul states,

It (reason) considers results and takes account of the fixed end of technique-efficiency. It notes what every means devised is capable of accomplishing and selects from the various means at its disposal with a view to securing the ones that are the most efficient. And here reason appears clearly in the guise of technique.[92]

In fact, this obsession with efficiency has transformed a variety of areas within human life. For instance, stress on efficiency has altered the notion of beatuy and morals. Prior to the dominance of efficiency, "aesthetic considerations are gratuitous and permit the introduction of usefulness into an eminently useful and efficient apparatus."[93] Efficiency had been understood as just one of factors taken into account along with pleasure, beauty, and goodness. Ellul accounts for the shift of this perception in illustrating the disappearance of decorations on such devices as sewing machines and tractors in the 19th century. Those machines had been decorated with shapes of flowers and bulls' heads, but later those aesthetic designs became considered gratuitous.

> The machine can become precise only to the degree that its design is elaborated with mathematical rigor in accordance with use. And an embellishment could increase air resistance, throw a wheel out of balance, alter velocity or precision. There was no room in practical activity for gratuitous aesthetic preoccupations. The two had to be separated. A style then developed based on the idea that the line best adapted to use is the most beautiful.[94]

Such aesthetic consideration for machines is regarded as running against efficiency. The press for efficiency puts more weight on knowledge calculated and measured than on human intuition and relational knowledge. The technological society forces us to pursue maximum efficiency. And efficiency becomes the single criterion by which technique is measured.

Empahsis on efficiency favors speed and effectiveness over moral virtues such as discernment, wisdom, humility, and authenticity, which require organic community life.[95] In this penchant towards efficiency, measurement supplants meaning by fostering statistical analysis and emphasizing measurable causes and effects.[96] The critical downside of the efficiency-oriented society lies in the tendency to reduce human communication to a machine-

---

[92]Ibid., 22.
[93]Ibid., 73
[94]Ibid.
[95]Schultze, *Habits of the High-Tech Heart*, 23.
[96]Ibid., 32.

like system for sending and receiving messages.[97] Thus communication has becomes a momentary transmission of information, with no bearing upon the context. This framework of the efficiency-driven technological culture has been also accounted for a reduction of the dimension of human communicating to a simple transmission of given message in a fast and effective way.

Communication that can be Standardized

It has been suggested that the printing technology is conducive to standardization. It seems natural that the preoccupation with efficiency leads to standarization by overlooking individual difference. Eventually technology comes to encompass every aspect of human life by rationally controlling and predicting it. Thus expanding rationalization in combination with the myth of technology begins to cover the entire society and its cultural forms. In a fragmented society, the belief in technology becomes a sole factor in controling human behavior and thought, and integrating every social form.

The technological system performs a dual role in deconstructing human life by way of fragmentation and reconstructing them according to the technological principle on the one hand and seeking to homogenize the value of human life on the ground of efficiency on the other. Such standarization can be compared to globalization without substantive meaning. George Ritzer argues that this globalization process resonates with the deficit of substantive and creative content based upon the local, which he terms "nothing." He states,

> "(G)lobalization and nothing (at least in the sense of centrally conceived and controlled forms that are substantively largely empty) go hand in hand. By definition, it is easier to globalize that which is centrally conceived and controlled. Conversely, it is much more difficult to globalize that which is locally conceived and controlled. . . . The main reason is that that which has much content also offers much that has the potential not to fit into, even conflict with, aspects of other cultures around the world; the more the content, the greater the chance that some phenomenon will not fit or be accepted.[98]

Clearly, the standarization of methods for human behavior and thought prevails in a society enamored with technological rationalism. This penchant for standardization, further creates a belief that the transfer of a message in a logical and straighforward manner is entirely possible, because communication is to be accomplished on a universal basis regardless of contextual variables.

---

[97]Ibid., 40.

[98]George Ritzer, *The Globalization of Nothing* (Thousand Oaks, CA: Pine Forge, 2004), xii. Ritzer's assessment of globalization process goes into details in rigorously theoretical analyses of subprocesses like "glocalization" and "grobalization" to delineate the globalization phenomenon throughout the world in more details at the ensuing argument.

A Linear Model of Communication

In a technological system, the process of production and the procedure for bringing out finished products are simple and based on a straightforward mode of communication. As compared to the organic worldview, which looks at things in an interrelated way, it may be the case that the mechanistic worldview resonates with a simplistic, straightfoward conception of communication.

In terms of communication style, the mass media activiely employs a mechanistic, sender-receiver model and assumes that audiences are relatively passive and easily affected by print and broadcast messages. Despite the ability of human beings to creatively interact in given situations, this approach assumes that communication consists in senders crafting a message and audiences receiving the given message in a simple cause-effect system. Thus communication has been reduced to a mechanical process of sending and receiving messages with the assumption that the message is mechanically transmitted to the receiver, once it is presented in a rationally coherent and logical way.

From the onset, scientific reason and technology were inseparable. Phrased more directly, technology builds on scientism--which attempts to organize society and control human behavior on a rational basis. The press for controlling and calculating human actions in communication is grounded in a linear concept of message transmission, which stems from the Enlightenment belief in logical consistency. The assumption made here is that as long as a message is transported in a logically consistent maner, a straightforward and predictable consequence is expected.

This critique is not to suggest that technology itself is to be discarded. There are numerous gratifying aspects to technological advancement which may improve the human condition. Highlighting the modern orchestra as a result of high technology, Ong issues an warning against condemning technology across the board. "Technologies are artificial, but (paradox again) artificiality is natural to human beings. . . . The use of a technology can enrich the human psyche, enlarge the human spirit, intensify its interior life."[99] In spite of such benifits, the effects of a technological culture must be honestly faced in order to understand and how it potentially changes the mode of communication which lies at the heart of evangelistic activity.

An Assessment of Evangelism Shaped by Technological Culture

The influence of the mechanistic perspective has been prevalent in all aspects of life and the technological culture formulated its utmost values upon a drive for fragmentation, efficiency, standardization, and a linear model of logic.

---

[99]Ong, 83

The church has been no exception to this general trend, and a vestige of this technological system can be seen in the practical activities of evangelism.

This section will wrestle with the technological elements of evangelistic communication by critically assessing literature and practical models of evangelism. This will not attempt to comprehensively cover the key patterns of evangelism models, rather it will focus on how technological aspects impact understanding of evangelism that may point to the importance of relational or contextual aspects. Thus this phase will set the stage for the need to address evangelism in a wider perspective.

Having established the four distinctive characteristics of communication technology: fragmentation, efficiency, standardization, and linearity, now we will explore how those aspects affect the ways we communicate the Christian gospel.

The Fragmentation of Evangelistic Activities

One of the problems many evangelistic models are faced with is that evangelistic efforts are disengaged from other areas of Christian life and church practiceses. Despite the fact that, in some churches, evangelism may be pursued as the primary goal of all church activities, evangelism is often treated as a separate department of ministry.

It is reasonable, to some degree, to maintain a distinctive ministry group that intentionally seeks evangelistic activities apart from other church ministires such as fellowship, worship committee, social ministry, and the like. These different activities have particular concerns and tasks in the life of the church. What is significant is whether evangelism has any bearing upon on other aspects of ministry and whether evangelism is pursued in harmony with other practices of the church. The effect of evangelistic communication is enhanced by its close connection tothe whole life of the church.

Thom Rainer narrates his experience as a visitor to a church experiencing a decline in numbers. His visitation was in response to the church leaders' request for a consultation that included an observation of the morning worship service. The church is evangelical and professes to be a friendly church. However, what Rainer observed when he visited that church was a loss of the spirit of hospitality, unavailability of parking space for visitors, half-hearted greeting of ushers, the unsatisfactory quality of music, and occupied seats in the back that would force new comers to make their way uncomfortably toward an unoccupied seat towards the front. Moreover, after the service, Rainer found it hard to engage in conversation with anyone in that church, because every conversation was dominated by existing church members who appeared to have little concern for visitors.[100]

---

[100]Thom S. Rainer, *Surprising Insights from the Unchurched and Proven Ways to Reach Them* (Grand Rapids: Zondervan, 2001), 88.

While Rainer intends to point out is the importance of the first impression in attracting newcomers and the value of a "newcomer friendly" environment as part of an evangelistic strategy, I further observe the lack of connection between normal church life and evangelistic intention. What is evident in Rainer's report is the lack of connection among different systems in hosting newcomers to that church. While people at the welcome center endeavored to create a hospitable environment for newcomers, ordinary congregants seemed to be not particularly concerned with them.

In contrast to such disengagement of evangelism from other activities of the church, ecological thinking attempts to see a certain reality in the whole, not as a separate entity. Equally, evangelism as one congregational practice should be looked upon in reference to the other activities of a congregation.

The fragmentation (or disengagement) of evangelism from the rest of church life typically promotes apathy among Christians. While evangelism is generaly accepted as one of primary tasks for churches and individual Christians, many of parishners do not feel called to directly participate in evangelism. Therefore, the many Christians do not perceive themselves as being gifted with evangelism.

It was argued in the Church Growth literatures that approximately 5 to 10 percent of active church members are gifted evangelistically to persuade the non-believers to make decision to follow Christ, while others may have the gifts of pastor or missionary.[101] This remark reflects two typical problems that relate to the marginalization of evangelism. First, it runs counter to the reality that communication brings multiple channels of human sense into play. Oral presentation of the gospel is not a sole criterion to assess the evangelistic gift. In commucating a message, there is a variety of ways to make its meaning known and felt. Thus, it fails to acknowledge the ways in which every aspect of Christian life retains an evangelistic dimension. Second, by legitimizing apathy towards evangelism for a majority of evangelical Christians, this notion may exacerbate the tendency for evangelism to become one disconected element among a variety of church programs.

Efficiency-Based Evangelism

In a technological setting that stresses efficiency, speed of service and convenience to achieve a maximum result at a minimum cost evangelism takes on a particular character. Pursuit of efficiency in evangelism leads to a dependence upon quick-fix prepackaged methods of presenting the gospel, since "the key to efficiency in the business world is being able to process as

---

[101] C. Peter Wagner, *Your Spiritual Gifts Can Help Your Church Grow* (Ventura, CA: Regal Books, 1994), 160. In this book, Wager presents the twenty seven gifts including the gift of evangelists.

many people as easily possible."[102] Efficiency in evangelism pursues the optimum means to an end, seeks successfully tried and tested techniques, and imitates neatly-prepackaged manuals for ready-for-use. It can be easily demonstrated that conferences, workshops, and program materials of successful churches give clients specific formulas designed to replicate their experience and reinforce the message that the formula works.

A simple formularization of the Christian message is a sailent feature of these globalized evangelistic programs. Their simplicity allows church leaders and parishioners to master a gospel presentation method relatively easily. Regarding communication used in popular evangelism methods such Evangelism Explosion, Ellenberger points to its simple, easy-to-follow formula, "It is the relative ease with anyone can go from trainee to witness to trainer, using basically the same materials, that gives Evangelism Explosion its transmittable strength."[103] This simpliticity and efficiency is often touted as an effective method for overcoming "a limited reach into broad populations, which equals slow progress in achieving the Great Commission."[104] Therefore, characteristic aspects of technological society such as efficiency with its simplicity and rapidity, are taken as advantagous to the practice of evangelism. This does not mean that we should discredit those evangelism models which value efficiency, but rather that we should seek an accurate awarenss of the technological factors embedded in such models.

The Alpha course, which is widespread throughout England and North America, has been criticized for its over-emphasis on the virtues of efficiency. Alpha manuals set out in great detail exactly how the Alpha course should be run: the strucutre of Alpha talks (lectures to facilitate conversation), the sample time table for each evening and weekend retreat, descriptions of the roles for Alpha volunteers and staffs, and supply of recipes for common meal, which has been vital to running Alpha in a comfortable way.[105] This offering of prepackaged curricula is often considered to be one of the reasons Alpha has been so popular.

One question about Alpha emerges with regards to the role of efficiency in a technological culture. Does such scrupulous and all-inclusive presentation of the Alpha course not come from our preoccupation with efficiency, which further prevents us from delving creatively into the detailed matters

---

[102]John Drane, *The McDonaldization of the Church: Consumer Culture and the Church's Future* (Macon, GA: Smyth & Helwys Publishing, 2001), 43.

[103]John D. Ellenberger, "Evangelism Explosion and Communication: A Response," *Evangelical Missions Quarterly* (July, 1997), 305. Here Ellenberger offers a fair assessment of Evangelism Explosion for its contributions and challenges. One area of concern he notes is that Evangelism Explosion might be in danger of neglecting cultural sensitivity if it adheres to the original form of gospel presentation.

[104]O. S. Hawkins, "Reaching all the Nations: Lessons for the Next Stage of World Evangelism," *Evangelical Missions Quarterly* (July, 1997), 303.

[105]Pete Ward, "Alpha – the McDonaldization of Religion?" *ANVIL* Vol. 15 (No 4, 1998): 281.

appropriate to the particular context? Since the Alpha course has been successfully tried and tested in a certain context, it is assumed (in an efficiency based culture) that the uncritical acceptance of its curriculum is an efficient choice when compared to the time consuming and demanding task of developing a contextualized model.

Over against this efficiency-oriented approach, the process required for a change in human behavior is more complex. Human behavior is rooted in character, and character is built from a myriad of small choices and events over time.[106] Every action should be sensitive to context in which the action is engaged. Since the consideration of context requires time and creativity, it is too often the case that the development of an indigenized plan of evangelism is ruled out by the adoption of the quick-fix prepackaged methods, which are proven to be effective in other settings, and aided by technological efficiency. Evangelism within an efficiency oriented culture is likely to be reduced to simple formulas and the universally applicable methods for evangelism prevails.

The pre-packaged models adopted to promote church growth are susceptible to exaggerated claims that particularly successful church programs can guarantee the same growth and success as has occurred elsewhere. It has been widely observed that the radical shift towards a contemporary style of worship is one of the surest strategies to revitalize the life of the church and contribute to its numerical growth by attracting the younger generation. Some surveys show, however, that it is not certain how important outreach events such as revival meeting, retreat, and the like are to leading people to Christian faith.[107]

Furthermore, sometimes we discover results which run contrary to the widely assumed explanations. For example, the explosive growth of Willow Creek Community Church is assumed to be a result of its innovative design of seeker sensitive worship. For this reason, it has become a model for numerous churches to follow. However, long before the emergence of Willow Creek's seeker sensitive worship, there had been some astute efforts to capture the minds of the unchurched and various attempts at using visual images and dramatic elements in worship.

---

[106] Howard A. Snyder with Daniel V. Runyon, *Decoding the Church: Mapping the DNA of Christ's Body* (Grand Rapids: Baker, 2002), 39. Snyder here brings a call for renewal of the church based on complexity theory that challenges linear system of thought. However, as regards the relationship between human behavior and character which is understood as mutually influencing in complexity theory, he favors an assertion that behavior is formed by character. His assertion is based on Jesus' words in Matthew 12:34b. "For out of the abundance of the heart the mouth speaks."

[107] According to Barna Research Group's survey of patterns by which the newly converted Christians come to faith, only out of every ten believers who makes a decision to follow Christ does so in church services or outreach events. Instead, a majority of salvation decisions come to being by way of personal relationship with a family member or friend. www.barna.org

In the pragmatic milieu idiosynratic to American culture, the styles of youth ministry since 1940's included fast-paced songs, skits, games, and the like with careful design of the whole procedure of worship as indicated in Young Life's Leaders' Manual.[108] The goal of youth ministry was then tailored to "make the students as relaxed as possible to break down barriers and earn the right to be heard."[109] Willow Creek's seeker service successfully employed such programs to address the needs of people in their context. The historian Michael S. Hamilton affirms that Willow Creek finds its own uniqueness in the particular circumstances and has built a ministry to meet those circumstances. He notes,

> For a century now, self-confident preachers have been willing to reinvent church in order to appeal to the unchurched. They have used nonsacred architecture, innovative, worship services, popular music, drama, and diverse programming to meet the needs of people who felt unwelcome in traditional churches. And a few of these new churches--to the surprise and dismay of the traditionalists--grew really large.[110]

One of the problems poised by this technological approach to church programs including evangelism is the lack of reflection upon context and, as a consequence, an absence of creativity in developing contextualized programs. It is grounded in the assumption that, like a machine, any successful evangelism program, "is pretty much the same everywhere, with interchangeable parts."[111] The church also is assumed to function as a machine. Another pseudo value that blurs some of the shortcomings of efficiency oriented evangelism is an approach to evangelism that ascertains the effect of evangelism by way of a measurable standard.

Standardization of Methods

Standardization of certain successful evangelism programs has become more common in the past decades. Numerous churches purchase the materials of successful programs in an attempt to replicate their success in attracting new members by following those proven models. This movement to replicate effective programs is not limited to the Western context. More widely known in the context of North American or European ministry, these

---

[108]Todd E. Johnson, "Truth Decay: Rethinking Evangelism in the New Century" Carl Braaten ed. *The Strange New World of the Gospel* (Grand Rapids: Eerdmans, 1997), 124.

[109]Ibid.

[110]Michael S. Hamilton, "Willow Creek's Place in History," *Christianity Today* (13 November 2000), 64. In addition to focusing on Willow Creek's seeker sensitive style, Hamilton points to the social and historical factor that gave rise to the mega-size nondenominational community church like Willow Creek.

[111]Snyder, *Decoding the Church*, 37.

evangelistic models exemplify an emerging phenomenon around the world of the globalization of successful Western world based ministries.[112]

At the heart of standarization and universalization is a commitment to assessing human actions and relations in terms of measurable quantity. Literature dealing with models of effective evangelism dwell mostly on the cases that claim numerical success that are also easily assessible.

Technological measuring systems require the whole society to evaluate the values of human life in light of quantification. Thus, quantative measurement has been overwhelmingly familiar to us as we have attempted to evaluate everything in a mathematic and visible way. Many churches and pastors spare no effort in learning and importing the practical methods employed by churches that have proven to be successful in terms of gaining numbers. Once a certain evangelistic or nurturing program is deemed successful, it will soon become widespread--even across cultural boundaries. However, such globalization of carefully developed, effective, simple-to-administer evangelism and discipleship ministry will be seen in a more critical light when we take into account the standardizing tendency of technological principles. To put this in terms of evangelism, the issue is that a prolific diffusion of certain models may threaten the content that is part of the local cultural tradition. While widely disseminated programs provide us with easy access to successful cases and ready-made tools, they may leave us without space for engaging in our own particular cultural and spiritual needs.

In line with standardization, evangelistic activities are often supported by the view that religious transformation of a human person can be controlled and predicted by carefully designed skills and programs. Drane makes a critical case against such emphasis on predictability in carrying out church mission and evangelism. He asserts that promoting the sameness of belief may

---

[112] Good examples of this standardization are Evangelism Explosion and Alpha. Each of these programs retains strong evidence of experimental success in its inceptive place and then keep reproduced in various places across culture. For one instance, over 5,000 Alpha courses are running in the U.S. and about 1 million people in North America have participated. Also, an Alpha video presided by Nikki Gumble is currently playing in one of 25,000 churches worldwide and over 5 million people in 124 countries have come to listen to his talk since 1980. For a recent statistics of Alpha course movement, see Debra Bendis, "ABCs of Faith," *Christian Century* (9 March 2004), 22-23. Evangelism Explosion makes obvious its intention to multiply its practical methods across cultures. With the bold vision of James Kennedy the founder of Evangelism Explosion in reaching all the nations in the world, it is even claimed that Evangelism Explosion already established its training ministry in all 211 political nations and made incomparable access to closed nations like North Korea. For evaluation of Evangelism Explosion, see James Kennedy, "Evangelism Explosion: 'Reaching all the nations' and its impact on world missions," *Evangelical Missions Quarterly* (July 1997), 298-301.

be deterimental to postmodern seekers who tend to place more weight on individual diversity.

> (T)he emphasis on predictability creates a constant pressure to homogenize all our understandings of discipleship and lifestyle. There is inevitably a temptation to process people so that they all turn out like clones of one another. The faith itself becomes predictable, and even experiences as personal and variable as conversion are forced into the same mold, so that in any given context one person's faith journey sounds much the same as another, because they have all been packaged to order, to fit some preconceived notion of how a "true" conversion should be.[113]

It can be demonstrated from the advertisements of certain evangelism programs that the success rate of winning converts is guaranteed to reach the high level. It is generally expected that, in most cases, a certain predictable result will come about if we faithfully follow the well-crafted guidelines and regulations of those programs.

Some effective evangelistic methodologies such as Alpha, which are tailored to people in a post-Christian society, have these downsides with all relevant strengths. Alpha is an improved form of evangelism in that it does not expound heavy theology, present the outlines of the gospel, and push the unchurched participants to make any decision on the spot. Rather it is administered in a non-threatening home-like small groups setting while touching on issues relevant to those outside the church.

In spite of these merits, Alpha appears to have been influenced by the principle of standarization by keeping " a close eye on how Alpha is applied 'on the ground.'"[114] In addition, Alpha appears to assume, according to its ten weeks curriculum, that conversion has taken place in a few weeks and after ten weeks a "fully fledged Christian is supposed to emerge."[115]

Chief among the evangelistic practices that conform to technological standardization is the tendencey towards a conventional understanding of one's spiritual stage as a uniform and predictable aspect of one's faith development. It would be worth critically reflecting upon stage theory in order to craft an appropriate strategy of evangelism as we come to terms with the problem of standardization.

It is similarly unwarranted to treat every one that is encountered in evangelistic efforts as being at the same stage. Ellenberger points out this dismis-

---

[113] Drane, 49.

[114] Stephen Hunt, *Anyone for Alpha: Evangelism in a Post-Christian Society* (London: Darton, Longman, and Todd, 2001), 35. In a similar vein, it is reported that Gumble emphasized the importance of not modifying the curriculum, while more recently the Alpha learners have been advised to tailor Alpha in minor ways to the needs of local churches by some Alpha officials. See Timothy C. Morgan, "The Alpha-Brits Are Coming," *Christianity Today* (February 9, 1998), 39 and La Tonya Taylor, "Adaptable Alpha Course Draws Praise and Worry," *Christianity Today* (November 12, 2001), 28.

[115] Ibid., 47.

sive assumption concerning one's faith stage as one point of concern regarding the communication style of Evangelism Explosion. "Methodologies that focus on conversion can easily assume all people are at the final stage of a decision and only need one last thrust of persuasion to clinch it."[116]

Attempts to judge one's stage of sprutual pilgrimage on the way to Christian faith may lead to a weakened vision for the diversity and complexity of one's spiritual journey. There have been numerous attempts to determine one's stage along the spiritual journey according to one's receptivity of the Christian gospel and to craft strategies appropriate to each stage.[117]

Looking at one's spiritual life in light of a pilgrimage model might help people discern their state of spiritual life and move on to a more mature stage. However, the best way to discern one's spiritual stage is known within the bounds of an accountable community which shares the spiritual journey together and is committed to mutual care for its members. In addition, one's spiritual condition can be assessed over time by the sharing community rather than postulated at the moment.

In addressing the development of one's religious faith, there are scrupulous academic delineations of the stages by which people come to religious faith. Lewis Rambo was a pioneer in spelling out seven stages for a religious convert to reach a religiously transformed life from context to consequence.[118] This analysis is helpful in that it indicates that there is process (momentary or gradual) in religious conversion, rather than a guage to locate one's level of assimilation toward Christianity as a static entity. The assertion that there are general stages in conversion needs to be understood as an impetus to consider the fact that people may pass through several stages and experiences as they move toward an ultimate decision for Christian faith.

This view of stage theory is not meant to suggest that such standardizing attempts be discarded completely. Rather it is my intention to suggest that this attempt to judge one's spiritual condition according to a rational scale is more closely associated with the standarizing tendency of technological culture than models suggested in the Bible which help people connect in differ-

---

[116] Ellenberger, 306.

[117] For example, Leighton Ford illustrates the spiritual decision process diagramed by James Engel and H. Wilbert Norton in their coauthored book *What's Gone Wrong with the Harvest?* This diagram categorizes human level of response to the divine call to eternal life on more than a dozen of stages. See Leighton Ford, *Good News is for Sharing* (Elgin, IL: David C. Cook, 1977), 86-87. Also, more recently, Thom Rainer and his research team scale faith stages according to the receptivity of the gospel from their comprehensive research of the unchurched. Thom S. Rainer, *The Unchurched Next Door: Understanding Faith Stages as Keys to Sharing Your Faith* (Grand Rapids: Zondervan, 2003).

[118] Lewis Rambo, *Understanding Religious Conversion* (New Have, CT: Yale University Press, 1993).

ent ways to the death and resurrection of Jesus.[119] Hence conversion involves a complex and dynamic process more typical to that in which human beings function. For example, stages of conversion are often better understood as having cyclic pattern rather than as being manifested as linear and normative model.

In the case of evangelistic attempts, this prejudicial attitude is often accompanied by a monologic style of communication, just as "the aim of conversation is to come to the point at which a gospel outline can be presented via a brief monologue."[120] Monologic conversation also tends to be built upon the presuposition of straightforward logic, which is largely dependent upon rational communication. This phenominon will be the focus of the following section.

The Linear Logic of Witness

Rational approaches to communication have been influential in modern evangelism methods. For example, Four Spiritual Laws (FSL) follows a typical formula of step-by-step logical development. FSL, as an official evangelism method of Campus Crusade for Christ, has been successfully used in drawing numerous people to Christ. Particularly, FSL was has been employed alongside crusade evangelism rallies.

FSL's plan provides Christians with a concise formula by which the gospel can be shared with unbelievers. Thus, it has the immediate advantage of challenging typical Christians to participate in practical acts of evangelism. Because of these clear advantages, thousands of witnesses armed with FSL have been deployed to campuses, beaches, shopping malls, and large gatherings.

When we examine the contents of FSL, we find that it is based on essential Christian doctrines presented in a compact way. The first statement is built upon the doctrine of God in terms of His attributes and His plan. The second describes the doctrine of sin--in particular the predicament of humanity separated from God. The third is about Christology which shows Christ to be the only solution to this human dilemma. The fourth is about soteriology--salvation is possible only by faith in Christ.

FSL faithfully follows a doctrinal structure based upon Christian theology. Also, FSL teaches that when the witness attempts to convince the hearer of his or her salvation, the witness should focus on the promise of the Bible in order that the hearer should not lean on an emotional understanding of

---

[119]Richard Peace, *Conversion in the New Testament: Paul and the Twelve* (Grand Rapids: Eerdmans, 1999), 293. Although Peace describes six steps of disciples' recognizing Jesus on his interpretation of Mark, those do not necessarily follow the sequential model of stages. He postulates, "While not every person will go through each of these six steps of understanding, by using these six titles as a way of talking about Jesus we make connections to people who are at various places in their understanding of Jesus." Ibid., 319.

[120]Peace, 291.

the Christian faith. FSL, as the most recognized evangelistic program in the world, has done much towards strengthening existing believers in the concrete content of the gospel as well as training them to be witnesses. However, its pattern of presentation and substance draws largely on the logical consistency of the gospel. This is not meant to discredit the doctrinal aspect of FSL. However, it might be asserted that FSL's brief presentation of the so-called "gospel outline" inordinately depends upon the capacity of linear logic. Also, its strategy is rooted in an expectation that a straightforward process of cause and effect will come to light. It is assumed that once the essence of the gospel is presented, anyone who hears it will respond accordingly.

With regards to this rational approach to evangelism, it is worth noting Alister McGrath's perceptive critique that modernism has been a key influence on the practice of Christian evangelism in the gospel presentation style.[121] Modern evangelism methods were designed in concert with a belief in logical consistency which is also defining feature of modernism. Under the umbrella of the supremacy of reason (as aggressively advocated by the Enlightenment), modernistic minds have infiltrated the reconstruction of evangelistic models.

McGrath decries the influence of rationalism over Christian evangelism in its emergence as a one-dimensional practice. "Faith comes to mean little more than intellectual assent to propositions, losing the vital and dynamic connection with the person of Jesus Christ."[122] Evangelism, as a verbal presentation of Christian truth in a cognitive style, is removed from the biblical witness of the communicability of the gospel, and is in fact closer to rationalism--which is a product of a technological setting. Technological ideology, thus, has managed to keep pace with Enlightenment rationalism. It could be argued that the modern style of gospel presentation is directed exclusively toward a cognitive dimension of our humanity.

In addition to this over-emphasis on the cognitive dimension, much evangelism is equated with a presentation of the gospel as a brief formula that captures the core statements of Christian doctrine. This presentation is usually arranged in an orderly sequence. It articulates and presents the core message of Christian truth step by step, and then challenges the hearer to decide on the spot. Apart from whether it is appropriate to encourage the making of a decision to accept Christ in such a brief time, the frame in which questions are presented runs parallel to a rationalistic assumption that a message can be fully communicated through a linear delivery aimed at a cognitive dimension. Given the assumption that communication consists in a simple transfer of information and that a message can be complete with the aids of linear logic, evangelism as a propositionally and objectively communicable practice becomes normative.

---

[121]Alister E. McGrath, *A Passion for Truth: The Intellectual Coherence of Evangelicalism* (Leicester, England: Apollos, 1996), 177

[122]Ibid., 177-178.

Another area of concern in relation to the shape of linear logic in technological evangelism is that it assumes that people are converted first and then later think about joining a church. It may be, however, presumptuous to say that understanding leads to belief, and once one comes to a belief, he or she participates in a Christian community. In fact, such a rationalistic straightforward sequence is not consistent with observable facts. Rather, the evidence from numerous cases that relate Christian witness and conversion, suggests that belonging precedes believing by leading people to conceptual understanding.[123] It is in the communal life that understanding and acceptance of Chrisitianity takes place over the course of time through shared experiences. This in no way is parallel with the linear logic of evangelistic communication.

Concluding Assessment

In light of the Trinitarian economy in history, at least two points can be made in a critical assessment of the mechanistic worldview as well as of evangelistic communication in a technological mode. First of all, contrary to the fragmentary and monolithic culture the mechanistic technology yields, the Trinitarian worldview manifests that all creation is embraced and interrelated in reflection of the Trinitarian relationship. The dynamic relatedness of the triune God is difficult to see in this mechanistic paradigm of thinking and practice. It follows that the Trinitarian theology moves us beyond the technological values toward a more plural and reciprocal communication.

Another area of concern is the loss of historical concreteness in evangelism. At the heart of evangelism is communication--since people cannot have access to the gospel unless it is heard (Rom. 10:14). In Scripture, the term "evangelism" (*euangelos*) is used to refer to Jesus' activity when He proclaimed good news as the mark of His ministry. Thus, in the Gospels, communicating the good news is at the heart of this orginal meaning.[124] Running contrary to the notion of evangelistic communication based on the concreteness of the gospel, much of what we do in a contemporary context to communicate the Christian message is strongly influenced by the mathematic operation of the world. Communication of the gospel is often understood in terms of conceptual transmission or program presentation rather than representing the life of Christ through the community of His followers. The Trinitarian plan for outreach to the world finds itself in the historical locus of the triune God's concrete embodiment. God's participation in the life of creation witnesses to

---

[123]In particular, Kallenberg reverses the logic of conversion emphasizing sharing with Christian practice that is followed by acquiring belonging and believing, and George Hunter also understands the principle of the Celtic missions in the fifth century as corresponding to the phrase, "belonging before believing." See following works: Brad Kallenberg, *Live to Tell: Evangelism for a Postmodern Age* (Grand Rapids: Brazos, 2002). George Hunter, *The Celtic Way of Evangelism: How Christianity Can Reach the West... Again* (Nashville: Abingdon, 2002).

[124]Jones, *The Evangelistic Love of God and Neighbor*, 24.

His redemptive economy and presents the way the community of believers has to faithfully embody. Thus, central to the triune God's witness is engagement in the whole dimension of life.

The aim of the present chapter has been to explore the development of the mechanistic worldview in the Western world and to to uncover cultural characteristics that emerged in tandem with technological culture. Its modest goal is to underscore some of the challenging issues that deserve attention if we are to avoid cultural pitfalls. In the next chapter, we turn to explore the practical wisdom, as an alternative thinking, to address these challenging issues by refining the technological mindset.

Chapter Three

Investigative Phase: Alternative Thinking in Ecological Terms

At the foundation of technological culture is a mechanistic worldview which disengages humanity from the world. Such mechanistic worldview has been challenged by other thinkers who understand the whole of human life and the world as an interrelated web. An ecological conception of nature and mind as well as a revisited understanding of communication in multisensory channels follows from this shift of worldview. This is the subject we will pursue in the present chapter as we seek to develop communication and evangelism strategies, which are concerned with the whole of life. Furthermore, this chapter will be devoted to proposing a revised understanding of communication grounded in an ecological worldview as an alternative to the mechanistic worldview. This discussion is preliminary to developing an enhanced view of evangelism beyond the bounds of technological culture.

Ecological Worldview

For several decades now, humanity has been aware that the deterioration of the global environment from water and air pollution, destruction of ozone layer, and global warming which are all symptomatic of an ecological crisis. This awareness has led people to be keenly interested in care for the natural environment and, furthermore, to recognize the need for a new paradigm in which we relate human life to nature.

Contrary to the mechanistic worldview, which presupposes distance between the world and human life, the ecological tradition advances a framework for understanding everything as part of an interrelated system. Every particle of the whole is interconnected with every other part. In this worldview, it becomes inconceivable to identify a single and identifiable cause behind every effect. Ecological thinking is borne out of this shift of worldview, and thereby lays the foundation for reinterpreting the concept of communication whereby human beings interact with each other and with the world. This changed view of reality provides valuable insight into how we approach human life and communication. It is out of this shift of worldview that the ecological conception of nature and mind and the revisited understanding of communicaiton in multisensory channels emerge.

Mental Process in an Ecological Context

The traditional dichotomy between mind and nature was prevalent especially in Western thought. While depreciating the split between body and mind so characteristic of Western culture, Gregory Bateson attempts to highlight the necessary interplay between nature and mind.[125] The notion that human life and the world are weaved into the whole fabric, reveals that we need to find "a delicate balance between the individual organism and its environment,"[126] rather than attempt to obtain mastery of the natural world. Furthermore, the ecological worldview requires the individual organism continually adapt to the condition of the natural environment.[127] Inasmuch as natural resources are interrelated with each other, the human mind replicates the unified biological structure of nature. How humans are related to the natural world and how other living things are interrelated are better grasped when we focus on how they are patterned after each other. Bateson puts forward the concept of "the pattern than connects" to understand the total biological world.

Bateson suggests that we take the aesthetic view, rather than rely on scientific observation, to find out how living things are related in certain patterns.[128] The shapes, forms, and relations of the biological world characterize the interconnection between the living things--including human life. Through those connections, humans also find themselves in tune with the natural world. Since the world around humans is systematically structured around patterns, it enables us to understand ourselves as well as our social organization.

> Man in society took clues from the natural world around him and applied those clues in a sort of metaphorical way to the society in which he lived. Then he identified with or empathized with the natural world around him and took that empathy as a guide for his own social organization and his own theories of his own psychology.[129]

---

[125]Gregory Bateson and Robert W. Rieber, "Mind and Body: A Dialogue," in Robert W. Rieber ed., *The Individual, Communication, & Society* (Cambridge: Cambridge University Press, 1989), 320.

[126]Robert C. Fuller, *Ecology of Care: An Interdisciplinary Analysis of the Self and Moral Obligation* (Louisville, KY: Westminster/John Knox, 1992), 37.

[127]Ibid.

[128]Gregory Bateson, *Mind and Nature: A Necessary Unity* (New York: E. P. Dutton, 1979), 8.

[129]Gregory Bateson, *Steps to an Ecology of Mind: A Revolutionary Approach to Man's Understanding of Himself* (New York: Ballantine Books, 1972), 484.

This insight into the pattern is helpful in understanding how meaning is defined. Bateson claims that meaning is regarded as an approximate synonym of pattern, redundancy, or aggregate.[130] For example, when it rains, we come to a verbal message "it is raining" through a series of past experience and current perception of raindrops. As experiences occur collectively and repetitively, a certain category of pattern comes to mind, and we come to define meaning through verbal messages. Where there is a connecting pattern, relevance takes place. Bateson explains this, "any A is relevant to any B if both A and B are parts or components of the same 'story.'"[131]

Ecological communication takes into account "resonance" in which an organism responds to the larger environment only when a pattern connects both. Resonance is a term used to define relations between an organism and its environment.[132] In this respect, communication is reciprocal and harmonious. The process of meaning making or relevance is important in communication, because organisms can communicate only what is meaningful and relevant because what is taking place is not a transfer of information or enforcing a message but rather the shared actualization of meaning. Such communication is what organizes and sustains the environment with which we are in dialogue.

An ecological worldview recognizes the fact that our species is part of an evolving environment and that human problems must be seen in terms of a total vision of nature, while Western thinking has tended to approach the world from a mechanistic basis. The world had been defined as a manageable and controllable machine according to the scheme of the dualistic tradition. In contrast, the postmodern age, (going through the so-called ecological crisis) asserts a communication paradigm that incur-porates the pattern of the natural process as one of the defining features.

The postmodern age is deeply connected to the ecological framework of thinking in that the former gives rise to the latter or vice versa. This is quite different from the technological quest of the modern age which attempted to gain power over nature for the purpose of human flourishing. Contrariwise, the postmodern age asserts that the operating principle upon which the interplay between persons or person and environment is based is communication rather than a control mechanism which asserts a linear system of cause-and-effect or straightforward logic.

---

[130] Ibid., 131

[131] Bateson, *Mind and Nature*, 13.

[132] Niklas Luhmann, *Ecological Communication*, trans. John Bednarz Jr (Cambridge, UK: Polity, 1986), 15.

The Nature of Ecological Communication

The nature of communication between organism and environment will be foundational to developing concrete applications for specific areas such as Christian communication and evangelism.

Relational Meaning

Ecological considerations encourage us to approach things in the world not in terms of fixed reality but in terms of relation. Equally significant and what gives language its meaning, is relation and context. Bateson deals with this contextual significance in conveying the meaning of language.

Most of us can remember being told that a noun is "the name of a person, place, or thing." And we can remember the utter boredom of parsing or analyzing sentences. Today all that should be changed. Children could be told that a noun is a word having a certain relationship to a predicate. A verb has a certain relation to a noun, its subject. And so on. Relationship could be used as basis for definition, and any child could then see that there is something wrong with the sentence "'Go' is a verb."[133]

The meaning of a word is not fixed, rather varies according to context. In this regard, the harmonious shaping of a word in context is equivalent to the pattern that connects. This relational approach makes communication vivid, since "all communication necessitates context, that without context, there is no meanings, and that contexts confer meaning because there is classification of contexts."[134] The various shapes of living things are legible only in reference to the connecting patterns of communicating, information, and message. The notion of communication therefore, is all about relation or context while keeping in mind the unity of the natural world.

Aesthetic Wholeness

This pursuit of relational unity, not uniformity, has an aesthetic dimension, because beauty is "responsive to the pattern that connects."[135] The movement of living things in the world cannot be fully accounted for by deductive logic because there is a more complex combination of rules, which are apprehended only through the aesthetic eye.[136]

---

[133] Bateson, *Mind and Nature*, 17.
[134] Ibid., 17.
[135] Ibid., 8
[136] Bateson, *Steps to An Ecology*, 409-410. Describing the notion of pattern as a way of looking at things, Bateson states, "To the aesthetic eye, the form of a crab with one claw bigger than the other is not simply asymmetrical. It first proposes a rule of symmetry and then subtly denies the rule by proposing a more complex combination of rules."

While verbal and conceptual languages speak to human consciousness, artistic expression is about communicating with unconsciousness.[137] Artistic language becomes significant in the web of ecological life in that humans have multiple forms of unconscious components and for these forms, artistic expression is more true to reality.

Aesthetics becomes important in the paradigm of ecological worldview, since an organic perspective looks at individual things in the world as part of a harmonious whole. While the mechanistic worldview tends to disengage the human from the world and mind from matter, the ecological worldview sees aesthetic reason more fundamental than the mathematic reason. Furthermore, in the ecological paradigm, authentic mental process is necessarily characterized as holistic and aesthetic. It is holistic because what make certain messages relevant and plausible are not separate parts of knowledge, but rather the total interconnection among the different parts. Also, validity claims are aesthetic because human reason is fundamentally rooted in its own sensual and material origin. The larger ecological and biological system consisting of animals, plants, and people is beautiful in that it unifies everything as a meta-pattern that connects patterns.[138] The human mental process must imitate the beauty of this natural process if the human person wants to remain whole.

Plural Interrelatedness

Since ecological thinking repudiates the linear model of the cause-effect system, it seeks multiple components that produce a coherent result. In the mechanistic thought frame, attention is given to the relationship of cause-and-effect. That relationship is well applied to machinery. If any input is given, a certain output is invariably expected. However, in considering the natural process and human behavior, at least three (and possibly many more) components are at work.[139] This notion of plural components in the process of human thought and behavior also lays a foundation for constructing multiple systems to facilitate human development.

As a consequence of an ecological crisis, there arose a need for a new paradigm of thinking built on the premise that all the living things exist in a complex web. This leads us to conclude that there are patterns that connect living things in the world. The ecological perspective impacts the ways in which the social sciences understand human development and the communicative modes of human interactions. This study will particularly focus on ecological aspects of communication and human development in order to reformulate evangelism in systemic terms.

---

[137] Ibid., 137
[138] Ibid., 17-18.
[139] Ibid., 135.

Applications of Ecological Worldview

In what follows, I will delineate how ecological thinking about the world as an integrative system can be applied to the areas of our concern: namely human development and communication. These two areas also correspond to conversion and evangelism, since conversion can be understood as a human development and evangelism can be understood a communicative activity without being equated. Thus ecological inquiries directed towards human development and communication will set the stage for understanding conversion and evangelism in an ecological sense.

The Systems Approach to Human Development

An ecological perspective on human development takes account of how various aspects of internal and external environments engage the process whereby people develop cognitively, emotionally, and behaviorally. This study is as concerned with examining life in context as it is in assessing the direct causes of phenomenal results as it seeks to uncover the variety of communicative components of evangelism. An ecological inquiry into human development, thus, draws our attention to the ways in which the interpersonal environment affects the course of individual life. It builds on the conviction that behavior, in almost any situation, is determined by multiple factors.

A responsible approach to human development recognizes how fully connected each and every individual is, not only to a larger social community, but also to a larger ecosystem within which human existence is located and by which it is affected (directly or indirectly). Bronfenbrenner and his colleagues have devoted themselves to this approach to the study of how human beings develop and respond in interaction with external influences.

Many attempts have been made to redefine evangelism in relational terms: friendship, life style, service, and the like. From an ecological perspective, such attempts (for all their merit) need more systemic complement. This is because they tend to delimit the concept of relation to a single, immediate setting containing the subject--which Bronfenbrenner refers to as a microsystem. Ecological thinking recognizes the fact that there is a variety of settings that affect human transformation.

Bronfenbrenner has directed his ecological explorations mostly on the cognitive development of a child within the ecological system. He asserts, "A child's ability to learn to read in the primary grades may depend no less on how he is taught than on the existence and nature of ties between the school and the home."[140] Even settings in which the person in question is not present can be significant to the development of a child.

---

[140]Urie Bronfenbrenner, *The Ecology of Human Development: Experiments by Nature and Design* (Cambridge: Harvard University Press, 1979), 7.

Bronfenbrenner contends that environmental events and conditions outside any immediate setting containing the subject can play a critical role in defining the meaning of the immediate situation for the person.[141] He further goes on to indicate the combination of multiple settings that impacts human development.

> The recognition of the possibility of relations between settings, coupled with the capacity to understand spoken and written language, enables the child to comprehend the occurrence and nature of events in settings that the child has not yet entered him or herself, like school, or those that he or she may never enter at all, such as the parents' workplace, a location in a foreign land or the world of someone else's fantasy as expressed in a story, play, or film.[142]

In this sense, the integrative effort is regarded as a necessary first step for the systematic investigation of human development in context. Human development cannot be explained by reference to linear variables but must be analyzed in systems terms. Thus, Bronfenbrenner first identifies four major settings that influence meaning making and development: (1) the microsystem, (2) the mesosystem, (3) the exosystem, and (4) the macrosystem. In his subsequent study, Bronfenbrenner began to recognize the need to address the effect of the temporal dimension upon the developing individual and developed (5) the chronosystem that deals with one's total life experience in socio-historical situation.

According to Bronfenbrenner, it has been generally understood that the most immediate setting might be determinant in the development of the individual. For example, the learning development of a child depends on the learning environment of the school he or she attends, or at the least the environment of the child's family. Bronfenbrenner opens up to a wider perspective to look at various and more complex and interrelated settings, which affect the child's learning ability beyond the direct, immediate setting. Thus he clearly defines the ecology of human development as follows,

> The ecology of human development involves the scientific study of the progressive, mutual accommodation between an active, growing human being and the changing properties of the immediate settings in which the developing person lives, as this process is affected by relations between these settings, and by the larger contexts in which the settings are embedded.[143]

With the foundational principles above in mind, a brief analysis of each system will unfold in what follows. This understanding of systems that affect human development will put the reader on an ecological journey that traverses every environmental domain from the micro- to the macro-system.

---

[141] Ibid., 18.
[142] Ibid., 10.
[143] Ibid., 21.

Microsystem

In Bronfenbrenner's work, a microsystem is defined as "a pattern of activities, roles, and interpersonal relations experienced by the developing person in a given setting with particular physical and material characteristics."[144] It is, of course, the aspects of the environment that are directly meaningful to the person in a given situation, that are most powerful in shaping the course of developmental growth . Nevertheless, it should be remembered that the developing person is not just a blank tablet upon which the environment makes its impact, but rather is a growing, interacting entity that progressively and creatively restructures the milieu in which he or she is located.

What characterizes the microsystem is that it concerns the environment perceived by the subject or developing person. The perceived environment is especially significant in that it is constructed by the developing person. However, in the process of construction, other environments can also play significant roles in developing the individual.

The various components of the microsystem come from reciprocal interactions between the developing person and significant others, objects, and symbols in its immediate setting.[145] In the case of a child, the quality of teaching in school, the relationship with parents at home, the level of parental support, and the like are within the purview of microsystem. These elements all directly influence human development.

Mesosystem

A mesosystem can be understood as a system of microsystems, which occurs when the developing person moves into a new setting. "A mesosystem comprises the interrelations among two or more settings in which the developing person actively participates."[146] There are numerous interconnections and social links, as well as formal and informal communications among settings. Interconnected relations between home, school, and neighborhood peer group for a child and among family, work, and social life for the adult are regarded with significance. Bronfenbrenner points out the effect of relations between events and persons on human development, even though the setting does not always involve the persons' active participation from the outset. For example, if we take into account the working importance of mesosystem in the cognitive development of a child, the relation between parents and teachers or parental involvement is also regarded as much important as the education quality of the school or the family environment.

---

[144]Ibid., 22.

[145]Stephen J. Ceci and Helene A. Hembrooke, "A Biological Model of Intellectual Development," in *Examining Lives in Context : Perspectives on the Ecology of Human Development* ed. Phyllis Moen *et al.* (Washington DC: American Psychological Association, 1995), 329.

[146]Bronfenbrenner, *The Ecology*, 209.

Exosystem

There exists another setting that indirectly but significantly affects human development, though the developing person is not directly involved in it. The exosystem refers to one or more settings that do not directly involve the developing person as an active participant, but in which events occur that affect, or are affected by, what happens in the setting containing the developing person."[147] This territory includes specific social structures and relational settings that affect the immediate environment of an individual, (but do not contain him or her), and thereby influence and possibly determine outcomes considered in this ecology. In the case of a child, examples of exosystem are the parent's place of work, a school class attended by an older sibling, the parents' network of friends, the activities of the local school board, and communities that have organizations for developing individuals.

For example, the parent's work environment may have a negative impact on a child's microsystem. If a parent returns home exhausted and stressed from workplace, it would be implausible for the parent to pay attention to the development of a child. In this way, although an exosystem does not directly impact the individual's development, it may be able to set a significant condition for persons to develop or make choice.

Macrosystem

A macrosystem is the most all-encompassing setting in which the developing person is (consciously or unconsciously) located. It is a worldview, cultural value, ideological belief, or paradigm, which influence the developing person in terms of everyday life matters including speech, deeds, and choices. It is interesting that even though ecological thinking builds on the loose web of life experiences without allowing for linear, directional system of thought, there is a kind of commonality in the ecosystem--which is the existence of a generalizing and organizing grand system, Bateson is confident that there is a meta-pattern that connects all patterns in which we live and exchange. This meta-pattern defines the vast generalization.[148] Thus he bemoans the fact that humanity has lost many of the core elements of life: religion, aesthetics, and great thought, while pursuing fragments of the ultimate reality.[149]

Chronosystem

In addition to these four subsystems, Bronfenbrenner includes a fifth ecological system to account for consistency or change over time not only in the characteristics of the individual but also of the environment in which that

---

[147]Ibid., 25.
[148]Bateson, *Mind and Nature*, 11.
[149]Ibid., 17-18.

individual lives.[150] Chronosystem, thus, is the time related change outside of the system itself. It includes the patterning of environmental events and transitions over life. Examples of this system are changes within the family, sociohistorical conditions, and historical developments within technology and its impact upon quality in everyday life.

An ecological approach will initiate the uncovering of different meanings lying behind those forms. Kurt Lüscher aptly makes a case that mental ideas are latent in metaphors, in rituals, in customs, or in other forms of symbolic expression.[151] Human development, according to this model, takes place through the interaction of various elements with multi-faceted contexts. Ecology involves all dimensions of human shape such as cognitive, emotional, relational, symbolic, and so on. It sees them in isolation and in their interconnectedness as well. In this regard, human beings are expected to engage in some interpretation as they respond to a situation or take on the task of development.

Organisms and environments are seen as influencing and interwoven with each other.[152] Lüscher suggests an interpretive framework through which "people attribute, deliberately or not, verbally or nonverbally, meanings to their behaviors within given contexts and to uncover the links in the chains of those (proximal) processes from the micro- to the macrosystems and vice versa."[153] Ecological systems approach is not just limited to a child development. It has been widely applied to assess the variety of human interactions such as domestic violence and fatherhood. This approach has proved helpful in unravelling the deeper interrelated components which result in problematic symptoms in human life. If human development is influenced from these different settings, the scope of communication needs to be enhanced to allow for this plurality.

Ecological Complexity of Communication

The emergence of the ecological paradigm impacts the way we interact in our communication practices as well as the ways in which we live. Marshall McLuhan introduced the concept of media ecology in his well-known aphorisms: "the medium is the message" and "the media as human extension." Although McLuhan elaborates on various media to investigate their characteristics and influence, the term medium need not to be understood in a narrow sense. It will be helpful here to clarify McLuhan's media "environment," "vehicles," or "external appearance of the content or message." For McLuhan,

---

[150]Bronfenbrenner, "Ecological Systems Theory," 201.
[151]Kurt Lüscher, "Homo Interpretans: On the Relevance of Perspectives, Knowledge, and Beliefs in the Ecology of Human Development" in *Examining Lives in Context*, 578-579.
[152]Ibid.
[153]Ibid., 579.

it is no longer possible for the medium to be understood as entity seperable from the message or subordinate to communicating of the content.

The new environment no longer accepts the use of medium as an instrument. Our use of any communication medium potentially has an impact far greater than the content of the communication itself. The process of watching television has a more significant influence upon our lives than the specific program or content that we watch. He illustrates the usage of the electric light to prove this groundbreaking approach to media.

Whether the light is being used for brain surgery or night baseball is a matter of indifference. It could be argued that these activities are in some way the "content" of the electric light, since they could not exist without the electric light. This fact merely underlines the point that "the medium" is the message" because it is the medium that shapes and controls the scale and form of human association and action.[154]

MuLuhan highlights the influence of media on weaving the fabric of human life. The change of media does not only mean the emergence of new tool for communication, but also affects the way in which human beings interact with each other. Therefore, the effects of media permeate widely our daily lives (conscionusly or unconsciously) in substantive content as well as in social form. In this way, communicative activities are ecologically integrated into the whole of life.

Though he elaborates on various media to investigate their characteristics and influence, the term medium is not used in a narrow sense as a technological tool would generally be understood. In fact, McLuhan's idea of media is far more diverse and holistic than the concept of media is commonly when used in a technological sense. By the using term media as a human extension he expands the defining limit of media to include the everyday life of human beings including such cultural artifacts as clothing, housing, printing, photography, automation, games, movies, and television as well as written and spoken words.

In the wake of McLuhan's thought on communication, Finnegan develops a theory of the multifaceted nature of human interconnections by attending to the variety of communicative channels that are accompanied by human senses. In particular, Finnegan endeavors to uncover a vast array of human senses such as sounds, sights, smells, gestures, looks, movements, touch and material objects which are used in communicating. Through this exploration, she counters Western ideologies that prioritize rationality and word-centered language in communicating. She assumes that communicating is not confined to linguistic or cognitive messages but also includes experi-

---

[154] Marshall McLuhan, *Understanding Media: The Extensions of Man* (New York: New American Library, 1964), 24.

ence, emotion and the unspoken.[155] Thus communicating involves a dynamic process of human interpretation rather than static transmission of a certain message.

Even when it seems that one channel of communication (such as speaking) is the only one being used, other human senses of communication like vision (facial expression) and other non-verbal channels are almost certainly in play as well. The process of story-telling is one example of this necessary combination of communicative channels.[156] Sound is in one sense fundamental to the process of story-telling. However, there are more than sounds in performance. Story is also conveyed through the teller's visual channels such as facial expression, tilt of head, posture, piercing eyes, head movements, and the like. In addition, the olfactory channel may play a part in a situation where the distance between the teller and the hearers is close enough. Sometimes, the tactile channel may be put into use when the teller invites the audience to bodily engage in actions like clapping hands with their partners. Even reading the book is more than just a visual presentation, since it accompanies the tactile channel through the materiality of the book.

What can be inferred from this multiplicity of communication is the significance of redundancy. Finnegan asserts, "Employing more elements than the bare minimum insures against failure."[157] In other words, drawing on more modes of communicative channels provides the possibility for a more transparent delivery of the message. Communication, when combined with other multiple channels in repetition, is effectively manifested and helps people reach a more profound level of experience. This integrative and multiple nature of the communicative senses is consistent with the ecological insight into how living things interconnect with each other in the natural world.

Conclusion: Benefits and Limitations of Ecological Thingking

To summarize, an ecological worldview shifts the way we look at relationships between humans and the natural world. This shift of thinking reveals how we interact with the natural environment and it affects how we exchanges message with others. Those characteristics that stand out in this ecological discourse are relational, asthetic, holistic, and plural. These insights into

---

[155]Finnegan, *Communicating: The Multiple Mode of Human Communication* (New York: Routledge, 2004), 5. Here Finnegan levels a criticism against the tendency toward a word-centered understanding of communication, which was a product of literary culture. A basic unit of our spoken and written language was the word. However, multi-dimensions are taken into account in holistic communication.

[156]Ibid., 227-228. Finnegan illustrates the fact that various senses like seeing, smelling, and touch are combined with the story teller's voice to make the delivered story real.

[157]Ibid., 236.

the nature of ecological thinking are more compatible with the Trinitarian theology than are mechanistic models.

Ecological thinking sets the stage for elucidating how we understand humanity's place in the web of life theologically. It generally evidences respect for the variety of social and cultural components more fully than do mechanistic models. It also captures the interdependence of human life and communication. An ecological map of communication aptly focuses on symbolic and non-verbal action.

Nevertheless, ecological thinking share limitations as well as benefits when analyzed from a theological perspective. First, ecological thinking can easily slide into naturalism excluding the providence of the trascendent Being. It tends to focus on the self-development of nature, while the Trinitarian vision is grounded in a conviction that human life and nature are supposed to reflect the way of the triune God's existence, and follows the redemptive economy of the triune God. Proponents of the ecological model often assume that nature has its own purpose and movement. Although it is true that the whole creation is ecologically interwoven, ecology needs to "fit into a larger story"[158] even in the light of radical ecological principle: any whole must be defined with reference to the larger whole. The biblical vision makes an assertive claim that all things cohere in Jesus Christ (Col. 1:17). "Jesus, as a person in constant multidimensional communion with God, provides the key to the interrelationship of all God had made."[159] Thus, the work of the triune God in the historic economy through the ministries of Son and Spirit is the fundamental interpretative category for understanding all ecological process.

Second, it follows out of this teleological naturalism that the ecological view tends to focus on the self-regulating and developing system of human life and nature. It has a conviction that development occurs by itself when the environmental systems run smoothly and harmoniously. Thus, all efforts are made to provide optimal conditions for natural human development. Maintenance of those conditions are integral to developing a human person. Although maintenance or good care (in contrast with neglect or carelessness) is central to healthy growth, a Trinitarian theology casts a more profound vision. The Trinitarian economy is destined for the restoration of the whole universe. Also, it seeks human transformation through being united with Christ beyond the innate development of nature and humanity. The work of the triune God through the focal point of Christ's ministry governs the whole process of ecological development.

Christians should challenge such proposed autonomous naturalism. We can admit that human beings should respect the intertwinement of the whole creation and that we are components of the larger setting system. On the other hand, it must be reminded that we as Christians participate in the divine mission of redemption and transformation by bearing witness to the

---

[158]Snyder, 123.
[159]Ibid., 131.

Trinitarian relationship and communication. The Trinitarian manifestation offers insights to the way we communicate the Christian gospel. Since the triune God created all things and embodies Himself in them, this presents the compelling reason that our witness to God can be enhanced and enriched in the variety of communicative channels and dimensions of human life. Also, the fact that God revealed Himself in the Incarnation suggests a more profound value than the simple combination of communicative channels. Christian communication of the gospel has a clear focus on knowing the truth. It is not only for having descriptive and subjective information, but also for providing a prescriptive framework to address particular human problems.

With this theological vision corrective to ecological thinking in minds, we move next to explore the theological mediation for understanding human development and communication in prescriptive terms.

Chapter Four

Correlative Phase: Conversion and Christian Communication

We have considered how ecological thinking has emerged as an alternative to the mechanistic mode. Also, a theological assessment about such new paradigm thinking was presented. Before engaging in the ecological systems model for evangelism directly, I will deal with the applicability of the ecological systems model for human development and communication in the area of evangelism.

Evangelism is carried out in a communicative activity, but ultimately aims at transformation of the human person. Thus, evangelism is closely bound up with the process of conversion, which involves more than assisting a person in human development. It helps the person join the Christian narrative of transformation as well as restoration of the whole creation including humanity.

As seen from the previous chapter, an ecological perspective offers the systems model as a way to discern how human development takes place. In order to correlate this ecological systems model with evangelism, two issues must be dealt with in advance. First, the meaning of Christian conversion needs to be assessed in relation to human development. Therefore, this chapter examines how the phenomenon of Christian conversion can be correlated with human development--which typically was the subject to study in ecological systems theory. Understanding conversion is foundational to how we do evangelism. If conversion is defined soley as a momentary event occurring through a cognitive process, the ecological systems model will not be easily applicable to evangelism, because this model has to do with the whole developmental process and considers multiple factors that result in human development. This chapter examines whether the proces of conversion can be congruent with the method of human development articulated by ecological analysis.

Secondly, since this study focuses on evangelism as a communicative activity, the present chapter also addresses the multiple types of communication found within the Bible and Christian tradition. The second aspect is also significant from the ecological angle, because it recognizes multifacted elements of human development found within the Christian tradition. Since an ecological approach connotes the interrelatedness of plural components in communication, the latter part of this chapter is devoted to showing how the theological vision casts light on such organic nature of Christian communicaction. This chapter will consist of a detailed exploration of these two premises in light of a Trinitarian understanding of ecological model. This discussion will serve as a catalyst for engaging the ecological systems model for evangelism in the next chapter.

Conversion and Spiritual Development

Before beginning this correlative discussion, it is important to note that while the phenomena of conversion and spiritual development can be paralleled to human development in formal aspects, they also retain their own particular qualities with regard to their content. It will be wise to deal with these commonalities and differences at the outset.

Conversion in a Developmental Structure

To begin with, the definition of Christian conversion must be presented in order to explore conversion with regard to ecological approach to human development. If conversion is commonly understood as a redirection of one's life or a fundamental decision for promoting oneself, it can occur in the process of human development generally. For humans to develop cognitively, affectively, or morally, it is necessary to have a scaffold on which to mount to the next level of development.[160] In this regard, human development requires some kind of conversion in order to move onto the next level.

In attempting to perceive conversion in developmental terms, sociological and psychological approaches to religious conversion will be of help in delineating the developmental stages or aspects. The idea of describing the life of faith in terms of stages or phases has a long history in Christian history. For example, a sevenfold analysis of spiritual development can be drawn from Augustine's monumental work *The City of God* as follows: (1) animation, (2) consciousness, (3) intuition of truth, (4) love of the good, (5) wisdom, (6) moral virtues, and (7) desire fixed on the highest good.[161] Recent attempts at describing spiritual life in developmental terms can be found in the works of such thinkers as James Fowler (*Stages of Faith Development*), James Loder

---

[160] Walter Conn, *Christian Conversion: A Developmental Interpretation of Autunomy and Surrender* (New York: Paulist Press, 1986), 26-30. Conn delineates the concept conversion plays a role in such qualities of human development as morality, affection, and cognition in a structural sense.

[161] Vernon J. Burke, "Augustine of Hippo: The Approach of the Soul to God" in *The Spirituality of Western Christendom*, ed. E. Rozanne Elder (Kalamazoo, MI: Cistercian, 1976), 10-11.

(*The Logic of the Spirit*), and M. Scott Peck ("the stages of spiritual growth" in *Further along the Road Less Traveled*).

The conversion experience is closely bound up with religious development, which also pertains to human development. Although definitions of what it means to be "spiritual" can vary, "spiritual development is human development conceived according to a particular set of concerns."[162] Spiritual development can be distinguished from human development as it begins only at critical turning points which entail self-critical and self-responsible growth.[163] Notwithstanding their critical differences in the contents of development, the quest for holiness in a religious sense is not necessarily antagonistic to psychological wholeness.[164]

Stages of human development have been explicated from different angles. There have been two general strands which analyze the human development from either a maturational perspective (Erikson's psycho-social stages, Grant's Jungian stages, Levinson's seasons of life, and Gould's transformations) or a structural approach (Piaget's cognitive development, Kohlberg's moral development, and Loevinger's ego development).[165] While the former focuses on ordinary, successive growth in a way which corresponds to each age development, the latter relies on the principle of organism growth in describing human development. Maturational approach highlights the unique, independent needs and value of each age development. On the other hand, structural theories of human development articulate a vision which looks to the whole structure of human development. Kohlberg understands this whole structure in terms of moral development. Piaget highlights cognitive development as the person reaches different stages of life.[166]

Conceived of as a particular approach to human development theories, spiritual development preserves its vital integrity. The relationship between human development and spiritual development is adequately described as symbiotic rather than mutually exclusive. Attempts to define spiritual life from a developmental perspective presuppose that religious development is human development conceived from a particular concern.

The works of Fowler and Loder describe the biological progression of a person towards spiritual maturation. While faith development itself constitutes the whole structure, they identify specific needs and spiritual goals for each developmental stage. These scholars, thus, provide a basis upon which we can account for Christian conversion as a developmental process. Accounts of faith development, along with human development theories, focus on age-related progressions and maturational stages in charting one's

---

[162]Daniel A. Heliminiak, *Spiritual Development: An Interdisciplinary Study* (Chicago: Loyola University Press, 1987), 41.
[163]Ibid., 38.
[164]Ibid.
[165]These theories are briefly summarized and charted in Ibid., 45-73.
[166]Ibid., 45-54.

intrinsic transformation. James Fowler's faith development can be seen as a representative case. He classifies six stages of faith development through the lens of human development.[167] The six stages of faith include intuitive-projective faith (three to seven years' age), mythic-literal faith (seven to twelve), synthetic-convention faith (adolescence), individuative-reflective faith (young adulthood), conjunctive faith (middle age), and universalizing faith (saints).[168] In this scheme of faith development, the Kingdom of God functions as the motive for spiritual growth of the developing person.

Loder surveys the situations and needs of the human spirit as it progresses into each developmental phase beginning with infancy continuing through the elderly period. He attempts to explore theological significance for each phase. For example, school-aged children are beginning to be preoccupied with achievement and social role. For them, a theological perspective can provide a fundamental grounding of human worth before the fellowship of the triune God, so children do not have to pretend to be someone else.[169]

Apart from analyses of age-related human development, there are also attempts to describe the spiritual journey itself. Peck refines Fowler's six stages of spiritual growth into four so as to describe the stages of mental health: (1) chaotic/antisocial, (2) formal/institutional, (3) skeptic/individual, and (4) mystical/communal.[170] Although Peck correlates his classification with a religious dimension, he is more concerned with the pursuit of psychological stability.

Traditional Christian theology identifies three or four phases as markers of spiritual development: awakening, purgation, illumination, and unification.[171] This outline covers the whole process of spiritual life in developmental terms. In a similar vein, Janet Hagberg and Robert Guelich propose an approach to understanding the process of spiritual development without age specification. They describe the various phases of the spiritual journey and

---

[167] James Fowler, *Stages of Faith: The Psychology of Human Development and the Quest for Meaning* (New York: HarperCollins, 1981), Part IV.

[168] Ibid., 202. Fowler is convinced that "persons who come to embody universalizing faith are drawn into those patterns of commitment and leadership by the providence of God and the exigencies of history."

[169] James E. Loder, *The Logic of the Spirit: Human Development in Theological Perspective* (San Francisco: Jossey-Bass, 1998), 195-196.

[170] M. Scott Peck, *Further Along the Road Less Traveled: The Unending Journey Toward Spiritual Growth* (New York: Simon & Schuster, 1993), 119-132.

[171] While Groeschel identifies the three phases of purgation, illuminative way, and unitive way, Loder puts the stage of awakening before purgation. Although Groeschel recognizes awakening prior to the purgation, he sees it as a precondition before the three experiential and developmental stages begin. See Benedict J. Groeschel, *Spiritual Passages: The Psychology of Spiritual Development* (New York: Crossroad, 1996), 72-75. Also, see Loder, 48-54. Loder interprets one person's story in these four stages.

illustrate how people act and think then in those stages.[172] Their six stages of journey are as follows: (1) the recognition of God, (2) the life of discipleship, (3) the productive life, (4) the journey inward, (5) the journey outward, and (6) the life of love. This stage theory uses sequential and cumulative terms to describe how people go into a deeper phase of spiritual life.

In addition to the above, there have been a significant number of attempts to delineate the spiritual journey in developmental terms. It can be asserted that conversion constitutes one significant aspect of the spiritual developmental process. However, there is a further critical point in understanding conversion than as in a formal structure.

The Theological Significance of Conversion within Human Development

Christian conversion is qualitatively different from the conventional and structural meaning of conversion in human development. Conversion in general seeks transformation. However, on a deeper level, Christian conversion has to do more with the content of conversion than the shape of conversion.[173] It deals with a shift of our fundamental allegiance in the direction of human life. It does not assume that human life develops naturally if appropriate conditions are arranged. Rather, the content of Christian conversion is determined by the object to which our radical direction of life is focused.

Fowler also understands conversion as signaling significant changes in the contents of faith. These contents are not limited to the values and needs of specific developmental stages. Rather they retain a structuring power to recapitulate the experiences of the previous stages in dynamic interplay. By allowing for this dynamic process, Fowler, attempts to balance his focus on formal structure and the structuring power of the contents of faith. The contents of faith include three major elements. The first are centers of value that give meaning to life and the second are images of power to which we refer the significant issues of life. Lastly, our faith is oriented by the master stories by which we interpret the events that impinge upon our lives.[174] Conversion, understood in accordance with faith orientation, is "a significant recentering of one's previous conscious images of value and power, and the conscious adoption of a new set of master stories in the commitment to reshape one's life in a new community of interpretation and action."[175] The process of con-

---

[172]Janet Hagberg and Robert Guelich, *The Critical Journey: Stages in the Life of Faith* (Dallas: Word, 1989).
[173]Peace, 6-7.
[174]Fowler, *Stages of Faith*, 276-277.
[175]Ibid., 281-282.

version, therefore, takes place in accordance with the entire span of human development.[176]

Broadening his scope, Fowler asserts that, "conversion can occur in any of the faith stages or in any of the transitions between them."[177] He also proposes the following six possible relations between faith development and conversion: (1) Stage change without conversional change, (2) Conversional change without faith stage change, (3) Conversional change that precipitates a faith stage change, (4) faith stage change that precipitates conversional change, (5) conversional change that is correlated with, and goes hand in hand with, a structural stage change, and (6) conversional change that blocks or helps one avoid the pain of faith stage changes.[178]

This description of the relations above suggests that conversion experience and spiritual development are encountered in dynamic interplay. On the one hand, conversion can take place in any stage of spiritual development. On the other hand, conversion can facilitate a spiraling movement of faith stages as it reconstitutes previous aspects of spiritual development. Fowler terms this role of conversion in human development a "recapitulation process." He states, "In the kind of recapitulative process I am describing here conversion would result in a re-grounding of these virtues and their reorientation in light of faith's new center of value, image of power and decisive master story."[179] Conversion, understood in this way, is not a disconnected side note of human development, but potentially can be a critical determinant which is integral to reformulating and reinterpreting the whole developmental experience within human life.

What gives Christian conversion its distinctive appeal is the radical turning of one's whole life to the covenantal providence of the triune God and away from self-grounded ideology for human flourishing.[180] This is the very "transformation" Christian conversion fundamentally seeks. It is transformation from self-grounded quest for human development to search for ultimate ground in the Spirit of God. The whole process of conversion is thus enveloped by the Trinitarian narrative of redemption. Conversion, understood in this way, is an ongoing process through which people participate in the Trinitarian meta-narrative which transforms and fulfills human life and the world in union with Christ. With this concept of Christian conversion in mind, subsequent discussions will explore the nature of conversion in ecological terms.

---

[176]In his comprehensive analysis of conversion, Rambo also concedes that "conversion can foster movement to a new stage of development." Rambo, 157.

[177]Fowler, *Stages of Faith*, 282.

[178]Ibid., 285-286.

[179]Ibid., 290.

[180]James Fowler, *Becoming Adult, Becoming Christian: Adult Development & Christian Faith* (San Francisco: Jossey-Bass, 2000), 113-114. Here Fowler borrows the biblical axis of "self-groundedness and covenant" suggested by Walter Bruggemann to describe the sharp difference between normal human development and Christian conversion. See also Ibid., 89.

Conversion and Spiritual Development as an Ecological Process

This study is primarily concerned with evangelism, for which conversion is the primary goal. If the conversion experience has a crucial importance in spiritual development (which is a form of human development), an ecological model for human development is also applicable to understanding how conversion takes place. An ecological perspective suggests that "parts are constitutive of wholes, and that the meanings of parts are determined relationally by their participation in the whole."[181] Building on this premise of ecological thinking, spiritual development and conversion (as one of its vital components) can be depicted.

Reciprocal Interaction in Spiritual Development

Spiritual development is, on the one hand, a form of human development and, on the other hand, an ecological process. Loder focuses on "interaction" as an integral aspect of a theological approach to human development. He argues that faith can not be purely and fully explained in developmental terms. Faith must be grounded in the gracious activities of the divine spirit, rather than on the developing ego's foundation.[182] Here, Loder proposes a relational, interactionist position to counter one-sided views of human development.[183] To him, development is defined as an "emergent resultant of the interaction between the person and her environment."[184] Similarly, spiritual development can be described as an emergent resultant of the interaction between the human spirit (as seen in developments of ego, morality, and intellect) and the divine spirit who repeatedly attempts to conform the developing person to the unitive will of the triune God. Understood in this way, spiritual development is congruent with the ecological process, since the ecological thinking also emphasizes the interaction of organisms with their environment. Neither the developing subject nor the environment outweighs the process of development. But rather, it is a reciprocal relationship between the person and the environmental setting.

In describing the stages of human development within an ecological worldview, Fuller employs the concept of reciprocity to account for dual modalities among humans. One example of this is the duality between activities to regulate the environment versus receptivity for adapting to a larger whole. It is through certain reciprocity between the two that interdependence of human life in the ecological system is established.[185] Thus Fuller argues, "The

---

[181]Fuller, 52.
[182]Loder, 31.
[183]Ibid., 19.
[184]Ibid., 20.
[185]Fuller, 35-36.

concept of 'stages' should not divert our attention from the fact that life is a continuing series of organism-environment interactions that rarely conform to neat theoretical models."[186]

This renewed emphasis on reciprocity or mutuality in human development does not mean that spiritual development requires synergy from both God and humans. Rather, the concept of reciprocal interaction is articulated in order to emphasize that the process of conversion and spiritual development should not be understood in a straightforward manner. This leads us to the next ecological component of the complex process and further from the linear model of the mechanistic worldview.

The Complexity of Conversion

Some articulations of religious conversion suggest that there are progressive stages or essential elements during which people turn to a certain set of belief. Lewis Rambo identifies the seven stages of conversion process: context, crisis, quest, encounter, interaction, commitment, and consequences.[187] Within this incremental vision, conversion cannot be identified with the entry point into a particular religious institution. This chronological and incremental view of conversion is in line with either the maturational or structural paradigm of human development. In this sense, understanding the spiritual life or the process of conversion in developmental terms is quite congruent with the ecological approach to human development. If conversion is understood as a developmental process, an ecological approach to human development is also worth applying to the process of conversion.

While understanding conversion as having incremental nature helps us avoid some of the problems associated with approaching it as a single event, such sequential steps do not always correspond clearly with experience. Although the configuration of human development unfolds over the course of lifetime and hence spiritual development can be depicted in developmental terms, the process of transformation ought not to be thought of in a linear manner. Gordon Smith makes a strong case that a study of conversion would do well to focus on the particularities of Christian conversion. Looking at the evidence through this lens would allow one to see that stages or phases may be experienced distinctly, but can come in virtually any different order.[188] Making use of Rambo's seven stages of conversion, Scott McKnight incorporates an interaction stage within the encounter stage. Also, he asserts that these elements should be called "dimensions" of conversion rather than stag-

---

[186]Ibid., 36.
[187]Rambo, 16-17.
[188]Gordon Smith, *Beginning Well: Christian Conversion & Authentic Transformation* (Downers Grove, IL: IVP, 2001), 145. Smith also specifies seven elements of a good conversion: intellectual belief, repentance, trust and assurance of forgiveness, allegiance, baptism, spiritual gift, and incorporation into Christian community. Ibid., 138-141.

es, because there is no guarantee that such components take place in order and one sets the stage for the other.[189]

In this regard, some analyses of the unchurched provide enhanced insights concerning the reciprocal aspect of human transformation. Both the Engel scale (as discussed in chapter one) and Rainer's scale (articulated below) offer useful tools for evaluating the spiritual receptivity of the unchurched. Rainer classifies five stages along a gospel receptivity scale: U5 (highly resistant), U4 (some resistant), U3 (neutral), U2 (receptive), and U1 (highly receptive).[190] Then, he suggests different approaches for people on different stages. For example, an apologetic approach and building a long-term relationship will be relevant to those in U5 who hold highly negative views of the church and the Bible, while touching upon heaven and hell issues may be more effective with U4. While such insights, based on the gospel receptivity scale, are practical and useful in implementing evangelism, due attention still needs to be given to the complex nature of human transformation.

Conversion deals with the experience of human beings in response to the grace of God. Under this rubric, forms of human responses can be taken into account in delineating the transformation experience. Accounts employing stages of conversion attempt to depict the variety of human conditions leading to transformation rather than the state of the person on the receptive scale. Regardless of whether conversion takes place at a specific moment or over time in an unfolding process, such components may be common to all conversion experiences, explicitly or implicitly.

Loder suggests that both the inner matrix (in which human development is embedded) and the outer envelope (by which human development is entrenched) are divine orders, even though it appears that human ego develops in the midst of sociocultural and cosmological contexts.[191] Nevertheless, fundamental questions about the meaning of human life inevitably arise and can be addressed properly with reference to the triune God. Thus, Loder places divine order at the center as well as the outer limit of the developmental process, and thus conceives of spiritual development as "a circumambulation of the human spirit around the center, who is the One triune God."[192] Recognizing the quality of this process supports the notion that developmental change does not take place in a linear cause-effect, but rather in a complicated web of settings. Such recognition of complexity can bring helpful insights into multifaceted elements of the conversion process.

---

[189]Scot McKnight, *Turning to Jesus: The Sociology of Conversion in the Gospels* (Louisville, KY: Westminster John Knox, 2002), 49.

[190]Thom S. Rainer, *The Unchurched Next Door: Understanding Faith Stages as Keys to Sharing Your Faith* (Grand Rapids: Zondervan, 2003), 20-21.

[191]See the figure in Loder, 75.

[192]Ibid., 74.

The Multifaceted Nature of Conversion

Understanding human phenomena as a process opens up a new level for exploring the complex realities of behavioral or cognitive developmental change. Ecological perspectives concerning human development are useful in augmenting the studies which see conversion as a process. Bronfenbrenner points to the crucial importance of process in ecological thinking.

> Likewise, ecology of human development builds on the assumption of process. Human development is the process through which the growing person acquires a more extended differentiated, and valid conception of the ecological environment, and becomes motivated and able to engage in activities that reveal the properties of, sustain, or restructure that environment at levels of similar or greater complexity in form and content.[193]

This concept of multifaceted process leads to another hypothesis concerning the more diverse and relational factors which make religious conversion possible which counters more linear conceptions of religious conversion which rely exclusively on a logical presentation of the message.

Conversion, in fact, contains a variety of stages and essential characteristics within its procession. McKnight highlights three orientations to conversion. Conversion through socialization means group membership, conversion through liturgical process means faithful completion of the process of liturgy, and conversion through personal decision means personal commitment.[194] These three orientations imply that the ecological process of conversion entails a variety of life events within social systems. While personal decision has been emphasized as evidence of conversion among evangelical groups, socialization and liturgical process provide wider perspectives on how conversion takes place. The ways of coming to faith are seen to be manifold and complex as we come to terms with these orientations to conversion.

Rodney Stark's study of conversion illuminates the significance the orientation of socialization in conversion. He reports that the majority of conversion cases stem from social attachment rather than from a desire to seek or embrace a coherent ideology for life.[195] Implied in this observation is the notion that people join religious organizations not as a result of personal decisions concerning doctrinal matters, but rather because of the strong social attachment found in religious organizations.

This argument appears to be more congruent with an ecological perspective of spiritual development. However, there is a missing link between how people establish socio-religious ties and how they come to accept certain truths. Even Stark himself concedes that, although the importance of doctrine should not be ignored, it plays a secondary role in being conducive

---

[193]Bronfenbrenner, *The Ecology*, 27.
[194]McKnight, 180.
[195]Rodney Stark and Roger Finke, *Acts of Faith: Explaining the Human Side of Religion* (Berkley and Los Angeles: University of California Press, 2000), 117.

to conversion.[196] Addressing Stark's argument in more detail is beyond the scope of this study. It is, however, helpful to recognize that religious conversion as a part of human ecological development can be greatly affected by a multi-dimensional view of the process of everyday life.

Numerous factors contribute to the experience of conversion. As such, more than one orientation can be influential in one's journey to Christian faith. While evangelicals have tended to focus on personal, conscious decision as essential to the conversion experience, conversion can occur at different points in various experiences. What is detrimental to the process of the individual person's conversion is "forced uniformity." McKnight issues a keen warning against the local church's alignment with a single orientation to conversion.

> When forced uniformity of conversion becomes a norm, a person's integrity, individuality, and identity are either questioned or violated. When this occurs, some persons develop what we might safely call "permanent religious adolescence." Instead of growing into maturity and spiritual identity, that person's own spiritual maturation comes to a screeching halt, full stop. To be sure, each church wants to see each person come to what it perceives to be adulthood, but in pushing uniformity onto the individual, that unconventional person may find the pushing so intolerably offensive that spiritual brakes are applied.[197]

We discover even more orientations to conversion when we consider how people come to Christian faith in other faith heritages. In some charismatic circles, for example, a person needs to experience a life-changing event in a mysterious way in order to be considered converted. Along with coerced conversion (as a denigrated form of socialization), transcendent experience is commonly understood as a powerful impetus to conversion to the Christian faith.[198] Such a variety of orientations suggests that conversion takes place in multifaceted avenues. Those orientations can coincide or overlap with each other over time in the process of conversion. "Some of those who grow up in a church oriented to a socialized type of conversion may need a more traumatic decision."[199]

---

[196]Ibid., 122-123.
[197]Ibid., 182.
[198]Ramsay MacMullen, *Christianizing the Roman Empire: A.D. 100-400* (New Haven: Yale University Press, 1984), 40-41. MacMullen documents a myriad of accounts to show that many points of contact with non-Christians came in part from miraculous encounters. Also see, Harvey Cox, *Fire from Heaven: The Rise of Pentecostal Spirituality and the Reshaping of Religion in the Twenty-first Century* (Reading, CT: Addison-Wesley, 1995). In chapters four and five, Cox attempts to explain the mysterious experiences common to Pentecostals to be expressions of primary speech and belief at the deeper level of human existence.
[199]McKnight, 181.

We can gain substantial knowledge of the variety of interrelated elements and contexts that affect one's spiritual journey, if we adopt an ecological perspective concerning religious conversion and evangelism. Any attempt to understand Christian conversion and evangelism, therefore, requires more than just direct observation of behavioral results. It will require examination of multiple systems of interaction (not limited to a single setting) and must take into account aspects of the environment which are beyond the immediate situation containing the potential converts. This conviction requires us to delve into the ecological aspect of communication in the broadest sense.

Multisensory Christianity

As was demonstrated in chapter one, Trinitarian discourse sets the stage for understanding the plural and relational aspects of communication. Also, the ecological worldview implies that all human phenomena are interrelated, and also that communicative channels are multifaceted and interconnected. The thrust of this section is to uncover the communicative aspect of Christianity in light of historical considerations. This discussion will prove to be important to counterbalance a tendency to communicate the Christian faith by way of verbal or literal channels.

In the word-centered tradition of Christian education and commu-nication, the literal has often been considered as most precise and desirable medium. "The age of print was immediately marked in Protestant circles by advocacy of private, individual interpretation of the Bible."[200] In contrast, compared to the word-centered orientation of Protestantism, the role of the visual or material has been overlooked or considered even dangerous to nurturing Christian spirituality.

The visual employs multidimensional senses by adding emotional and spatial dimentions to cognitive opperations. The rise of the image may, therefore, bring a more balanced perspective to human experience and knowledge then we experienced under the dominance of logocenterism. Miles advocates the complementary role the image plays, "We could begin to learn the language of images, a language that compensates in affective richness for what it lacks in intellectual exactness."[201] Visual images will likely help us new ways to receive knowledge and experience relationships.

This new emphasis on multiplicity in meaning making will help us explore the systemic view of communication in the reorientation of evangelism.

The Protestant churches have, nevertheless, been tempted to enshrine truth in purely propositional and rational form. "Theology was like the scholastic disciplines in which analysis, classification, prediction, and clarification

---

[200]Ong, 153.
[201]Miles, p. 34.

played a major role."[202] It should be noted, however, that the situation today has changed. The diversity of sensibilities is now fully accepted in the wider society. The pluralistic world we are living in presents a new opportunity to widen our modes of discourse in order to express theological conviction. Then "we need the discipline of each sensibility in order to express a full humanity eschatologically oriented to its fulfillment."[203]

The arts constitute a final product with its own language rather than serving simply as a vehicle for the word.[204] Bach's music, for example, contains an evangelistic implication apart from its embedded message. It is argued that Bach's music convey a sense of joy, peace, beauty, and comfort which could evoke in the listener a belief in ultimate beauty and elicits a certain openness to faith in the presence of God as the ultimate ground of beauty.[205] Artistic expression is crucially important in witnessing to the Christian faith, in that it requires whole aspects of human life to participate in the experience of the transcendent reality. In this regard, being a Christian is not simply a rational conviction about the truth of Christianity, but rather is an integration of truth, beauty, and goodness which must come together to grow and transform a person toward Christian commitment.[206]

Such an approach to evangelism is based on the premise that the text or content can be best understood with reference to context. It is often assumed that the context is at best complementary to the text. The value the context carries is secondary to the content to which it ultimately refers. As seen from the foregoing discussion, however, the relationship between concept and symbol, or message and culture (or everyday life) cannot be separated. In other words, a Christian way of life or cultural practice plays a substantial role in making the content of the gospel clear and reliable, because it is grounded in the theological premise that the revelation of the triune God has involved tangible and visual embodiments in human history.

---

[202] John Dillenberger, *A Theology of Artistic Sensibilities: The Visual Arts & the Church* (New York: Crossroad, 1986), 248.

203 Ibid., 249.

204 Richard Viladesau, *Theology and the Arts: Encountering God through Music, Art and Rhetoric* (New York: Paulist, 1989), 31.

205 Ibid., 45.

206 Brian McLaren, *More Ready Than You Realize: Evangelism as Dance in the Postmodern Matrix* (Grand Rapids: Zondervan, 2002), 66.

Summary

In this chapter we have explored the application of ecological notions in conversion and Christian communication. What insights do we gain from such ecological focus on the interrelatedness of developmental settings and the wider dimensions of communicative channels? We have answered that question by suggesting that we look at how conversion takes place as a multifaceted process. To look at conversion in developmental terms is to set the stage for the ecological systems model with respect to relate to evangelism, since how we view conversion determines how we approach evangelism. Furthermore, the Trinitarian focus in Christian conversion is significant for an inquiry into the applicability of ecological systems of human development for evangelism. Since humanity and all creation share the lost image of God, Christian conversion postulates that our transformation through the ministry of the Son by the power of the Spirit moves us beyond self-grounded development to participation in and communion with the Trinitarian economy. Conversion can occur in the process of human development by critically redirecting the process itself. A focus on Christian conversion functions as a threshold through which inquiries into ecological systems for human development can enter into a dialogue with evangelism in a Trinitarian perspective.

Also, we have explored how the Christian vision of communication allows for a rich diversity of human senses and avenues through which people can engage the message of the gospel. It must be noted that the triune God embeds this whole process since He reveals Himself in self-relatedness and also produces the world in a fashion that is congruent with His way of existence. Thus, a Trinitarian discourse opens up a way to explore multiple modes of Christian communication and points to the need for a reconsideration of the various settings for evangelistic processes. In the next chapter, I will pursue this agenda in more detail and delve into the concrete forms of ecological systems for a distinctly Christian communication of the gospel.

Chapter Five

Strategic Phase: Ecological Systems of Evangelism

This study has endeavored to demonstrate that it might be reductionistic to conceive of evangelism as consisting of one single factor or executed through one programmatic model. The Trinitarian shape of Christian faith and practice does not bear witness to such mechanistic modes of thought and behavior, rather it focuses more on the interrelated and harmonious way of engagement in the practice of evangelism. Every aspect of behavior, space, and style is important because the entire Christian community has a stake in the demonstration of the Trinitarian faith. In this section, we will explore, in systems terms, the ways in which the organic process of evangelism may take place. Before delving into a selected case of ecological systems in evangelism, it will be helpful to take a brief look at the systems perspective.

Systems Thinking and Evangelism

Systems-thinking has been widely employed in fields of social science such as psychology and family studies. It resonates with the ecological model, since it attempts to study patterns in complex interrelationship. Systems take a variety of shapes and functions. The more we understand the complex reality of systems, the less our model of thought will be mechanistic, linear, and hierarchical, and thus, will be truer to the actual praxis of life.

Systems approach to families or congregations is an attempt to look at and deal with those institutions as living systems. When one works with a living system, one deals with process, not substance, and connectedness, not parts. No single element of the whole is thought of as functioning independently of the other components. In other words, wholeness is relational.

Peter Steinke contrasts systems thinking with "separate parts thinking."[207] While the latter focuses on the individual, the former takes the whole into account. Separate parts thinking tries to explain whole by way of parts, but

---

[207] Peter L. Steinke, *Healthy Congregations: A Systems Approach* (The Alban Institute, 1993), 11.

systems thinking explains parts by way of whole. In the systems scheme of thinking, parts mutually influence one another rather than only themselves. Separate parts thinking builds on a cause and effect, linear model, but systems thinking opens up the great potential of co-incidence and reciprocity.

In such issues as marital struggles, if one were to focus on content alone, he or she would mostly likely look to one partner's personality, temper, or behavior as the source of problem, and then try to fix or blame it. However, systems thinking explores the larger environmental factors, such as one's relationship with extended family members that may be relevant. The problem is not dealt with at the surface level, but rather is solved by setting aside content issues in order to focus on the process or context in which immediate problems are situated.

In light of this framework of systems-thinking, an approach to evangelism necessarily must be ecological. An ecological approach is as likely to seek religious inspiration in various media and settings such as art, literature, architecture, and everyday realities as it would be in formal works of theology which directly relate to evangelism. The major point systems thinking establishes with regards to the practice of evangelism is to refocus our attention on the larger settings that engage in human transformation. It is often the case that evangelistic activity is focused on an immediate setting in which the message of the gospel is commended. But in an ecological approach to evangelism, our attention is shifted to other factors that are, directly or indirectly, involved in the larger context of evangelism. If we can accept that conversion occurs in a developmental and contextual process, then it will be significant to note how various settings or systems affect the conversion process that is critical to human transformation. In the ensuing discussion, those settings will be analyzed.

When Bronfenbrenner presents evidences of ecological systems, he employs a variety of existing research findings to establish his ecological theory rather than conducting his own research. His proposal is, therefore, built on collecting, reorganizing, and reinterpreting the existing research findings of other scholars (including himself) to construct the ecological systems model of human development. The focus of this chapter will be to generalize evangelistic facts in a framework of ecological systems rather than to focus on one specific case in detail. In doing so, I will scrutinize selected materials which report evangelistic results and, in particular, pay attention to contributing factors that may be better understood through the ecological systems approach. The materials will include personal stories and case reports as well as research findings that relate the enhancement of evangelistic communication. The ensuing discussion is not meant to be exhaustive, but rather illustrative or suggestive, in order to propose the applicable relevance of ecological systems to evangelistic communication.

Microsystem and Evangelism

In the ecology of human development, a microsystem concerns "a pattern of activities, roles, and interpersonal relations experienced by the developing person in a given setting with particular physical and material characteristics."[208] A setting here refers to a place where the developing person engages in face-to-face interaction. The elements of a microsystem consist of activities, roles, and interpersonal relations. The most salient feature of microsystem functions is that the developing person should experience the elements directly and be engaged by activities that are intentional. In other words, the microsystem for evangelism is closely bound up with the immediate setting that directly influences the potential convert. Bronfenbrenner makes inquiries into microsystem settings such as day care, preschool, and the role of significant others for childhood development. In addition to identifying the microsystem settings, he points out that intentional activities performed by parents, teachers, and organizations facilitate the development of a child. In the same way, this study assumes that faith development is directly influenced by microsystem components.

Though the microsystem analysis has been given due attention in planning and practicing evangelism, it is worth articulating the particular elements of a microsystem in terms of evangelism aided and abetted by an ecological developmental theory. Bronfenbrenner makes reference to the detrimental effects on children who are deprived of sufficient social relationship and physical contact with caretakers and parents. He then offers a hypothesis about the potential of human development according to a microsystem perspective.

The developmental potential of a setting is enhanced to the extent that the physical and social environment found in the setting enables and motivates the developing person to engage in progressively more complex molar activities, patterns of reciprocal interaction, and primary dyadic relationship with others in that setting.[209]

Insights into evangelism can be unpacked by working with this same hypothesis of ecological microsystem above. A microsystem in evangelism might have to do with endeavors and programs that directly engage in verbally or nonverbally communicating the gospel to those outside of the Christian community. Every practical model of evangelism can be developed and grasped within the purview of microsystems. First of all, evangelism has been and must continue to be understood as an intentional act of advocating the Christian message. Intentionality is crucial in distinguishing the dimension of microsystem from other systems. This intentional act is enhanced when it

---

[208] Bronfenbrenner, *The Ecology*, 22.
[209] Ibid., 163.

is accompanied by a diversity of roles and reciprocal relationships between the developing person and care-takers so as to yield the ecological conditions most favorable to human development.

Plural Avenues of Communication

Everything a Christian does can be assessed for its evangelistic potential, but not everything can be described as evangelistic from a microsystem perspective. What distinguishes evangelism in the microsystem from other kinds of acts and ingredients is whether a certain activity encounters potential converts in a direct, immediate setting. Evangelistic activities are distinguished from other activities carried out in the church, in that they fulfill their evangelistic purpose or evangelistic dimension by way of a Christian message. Intentional evangelism is not limited to any verbal or written presentation of Christianity, however. Rather, the direct means of evangelism can be found in a wide array of church activities as available means for communicating the gospel. By the same token, an inquiry into evangelism in terms of microsystem requires a variety of communicative channels including artistic expressions and relational interactions. The microcosm of evangelism, thus, takes account of emotional, visual, and relational approaches in addition to cognitive way of delivering the message. This approach underscores the fact that, the contents of evangelism are not necessarily confined to cognitive or propositional level.

The communicative channel of witness may take a variety of forms beyond the verbal or literal delivery of the gospel. For example, Michael Green illustrates the evangelistic dimension of decoration in early Christian houses. It was expected that the decoration and artwork within Christian homes bore witness to the Christian faith for pagan visitors. Use of visual image served as one of the main avenues for communicating a message in the ancient times. As Miles points out, in the early Christian period inasmuch as other ancient times, "relatively few Christians read theological treatises, but all participated in the community's artistic repertoire."[210]

Evidence of expressing their Christian faith through arts has been found in the archaeological discoveries of Christian houses in from Roman times. Mosaics and frescoes are found to have abounded in first century Roman houses. Likewise, mosaics and paintings depicting Eucharistic loaves, chalice, fish, biblical figures and stories, as well as praying figures have been found in such homes as well as in the Catacombs

Sometimes the motifs of painting and inscriptions expressed secular repertoires as evidenced in Orpheus playing his lyre, and Cupid and Psyche gathering flowers.[211] But it was often the case that Christians creatively and subtly

---

[210] Miles, *Word Made Flesh*, 4.
[211] Ibid., 58.

modified those common images with Christian themes.[212] External spaces (such as the atrium, vestibule, and peristyle) of the upper-middle-class Christian houses were often rich with mosaics of Christian symbols such as fish, rams, and even the occasional plaque depicting Jesus' face. It may be construed from this observation that those works of art were meant to function as a catalyst to facilitate a spiritual conversation.[213] Green touches upon the further possibility of evangelistic effect that such decoration might have made--though tentative and allusive. It is because such Christian decorations "would mean much to a fellow Christian, but would either seem unremarkable to the non-Christian or might excite mild comment, which in turn could give the Christian householder an opportunity to bear witness to his faith."[214]

John Finney accounts for the difference between the Celts and the Romans with respect to their knowledge and learning patterns. While the Romans stressed order and clarity in apologetics and evangelism, as wanderers the Celts loved poetry and reveled in color and design.[215] Scholarship and literature flowered under the hegemony of the Roman church. But, poems, songs and reflection concerning nature were subjects dear to the Irish people. It is possible that the effectiveness of the evangelistic outreach to the Celts in the medieval era was anchored in the pioneering missionaries' scrupulous endeavor to adapt to the cultural manifestations of the Celts and to develop a multi-sensory communication of the Christian message.

The Celtic evangelistic approach employed plural channels in communicating the Christian faith. To get the message across, it attempted to reach people through numerous encounters with the gospel. With regards to the microsystem perspective on evangelism, therefore, we can observe that evangelistic efforts may require multiple exposures to the gospel.

This ancient missionary approach suggests multiple ways for evangelistic communication to be diverse and rich. It also makes us aware of the possibility that every kind of human act, media, and living situation can be considered to be conveying a certain meaning.

---

[212]Michael Green, *Evangelism in the Early Church* (Grand Rapids: Eerdmans, 1997), 330. Green here illustrates two examples of *oranti* (figures with arms outstretched in prayer) dated around AD 79 at Pompeii. "For all their similarity, there is a striking difference between the pagan *orante* and the Christian one, which was evidently modeled on it. The former keeps the upper arms to the side of the body, while extending the forearms in supplication. The similarity to the pagan type would allow the Christian *orante* to go unchallenged by most visitors to the home.... and the pagan acquaintance interested enough to enquire about its peculiarities would provide his host with an ideal opportunity of explaining the faith to him."

[213]Ibid., 331-332. Green also challenges the notion that the symbol of cross was not used in the first centuries of the early church by showing some archaeological discoveries of Christian homes.

[214]Ibid., 329.

[215]Finney, 60.

In this regard, we can see that the wide arrays of communicative genres engaged in by the Celts are further justified through the case for audiovisual and symbolic ways of communicating the gospel that appeal to the postmodern generation who, like the Celts, are more oriented to symbolic and artistic language. Various ways of expressing and experiencing this Christian dimension are made possible in part through the use of symbolic language. Symbolic language speaks to the heart and the unconsciousness as we have seen in the chapter three. It guides the person beyond the visible material to touch and experience an invisible reality.

The microsystem perspective on evangelism concerns all possible immediate settings that would engage the potential convert. The presentation of the gospel is not limited to a cognitive proclamation. The communication of a message is not only carried out through the human mind, but also through heart and body. Non-verbal and artistic expressions are able to affect the whole person, whereas cognitive communication focuses on the cerebral dimension alone. In conjunction with this insight, the microsystem recognizes the multiple avenues of communication in evangelism.

Diversified Advocates

It would not be overstating the case to say that the role of the evangelistic agent continues to enjoy extreme significance. As the person attempts to move on to the next phase in one's developmental pilgrimage, the advocate often takes a significant role in facilitating this move. Coming to terms with initial contacts with people outside the church, an evangelistic advocate of Christianity can make a difference for people in a local church. In drawing people to a Christian community, evangelism is largely dependent upon relational connections rather than on effective advertising. The personal level of evangelistic activity is still considered important and necessary. Despite the problem of over-familiarity in evangelistic communication, what makes evangelism real and tangible is the commitment of persons who participate in various activities of witness. Assessing the church types with regard to holistic outreach, Ronald Sider and his colleagues point out that the most obvious reason why people come to a church for an outreach ministry but never return for worship is that they are not properly invited.[216]

This does not mean, of course, that everybody in a congregation should be trained to give verbal witness to the gospel. Rather, emphasis should be placed upon the responsibility every Christian has to the ministry of evangelism. The goal of evangelism training, therefore, is to help each member of the Christian community discern how best one's unique gifts can be used in

---

[216] Ronald J. Sider, Philip N. Olson & Heidi R. Unruh, *Churches That Make a Difference: Reaching Your Community with Good News and Good Works* (Grand Rapids: Baker, 2002), 114.

support of evangelism.[217] Contagious Witness (CW) curriculum, developed by Willow Creek Church, presents six types of gifts that help promote corporate evangelism for the local congregation. Contrary to the common assumption that only a small percentage Christians within the whole congregation are evangelistically gifted, the basic idea of this curriculum is entrenched by the belief that every Christian is endowed with a unique style and personality which equips them to take part in congregational evangelism. Mark Mittelberg makes the case that a diversity of approaches to evangelism can be seen in the witness styles of key figures throughout the New Testament. This includes such characters as confrontational (Peter), intellectual (Paul), testimonial (the blind man Jesus healed in John), interpersonal (Matthew), invitational (the Samaritan woman), and serving (Dorcas).[218] CW sees evangelism as a corporate enterprise which requires the whole community and cares deeply about the process over time. If evangelism is to be grasped as a corporate ministry that takes place over time, different roles and gifts are required to actualize that ministry.[219] Confrontational style refers to those who can confidently and clearly deliver the point of the gospel to the nonbelievers. Chuck Colson and Billy Graham are gifted with this style. The intellectual style fits those who engage in arguments and apologetics such as Josh McDowell and Lee Strobel. These kinds of Christians help "clear the way to the central Gospel message."[220] Testimonial style evangelists are clear storytellers while (at the same time) being good listeners. CW curriculum presents Corrie ten Boom as this type.[221] People of this type tend to narrate how they are reached by God at the personal level and try to link their experience to that of their listeners. The interpersonal style pays attention to making of friendship, sensitive relationships and other felt-needs on personal level in doing evangelism. Pippert's *Out of the Salt Shaker & into the World* and Joe Aldrich's *Life-Style Evangelism* involve this kind of evangelism. The invitational style fits those who like to be hospitable and meet people. People of this type may see "outreach events as unique opportunities."[222] The serving style finds biblical expression in Dorcas who (according to Acts 9) served the early church. This group stresses showing love through action rather than words.[223] Among contemporaries Mother Teresa and Jimmy Carter exemplify this group.

---

[217]Ibid., 77.

[218]Mark Mittelberg, *Building a Contagious Church: Revolutionizing the Way We View and Do Evangelism* (Grand Rapids: Zondervan, 2000), 156.

[219]Ibid., 247-338. Here Mittelberg presents numerous cases for each type of evangelism style that have been actually on the local church level.

[220]Mark Mittelberg, Lee Strobel, and Bill Hybels, *Becoming A Contagious Christian: Leader's Guide – Communicating Your Faith in a Style that Fits You* (Grand Rapids: Zondervan, 1995), 259.

[221]Ibid., 260
[222]Ibid., 262.
[223]Ibid., 263.

In addition to noting a diversity of advocates, Mittelberg endeavors to develop various models and practices of evangelism with respect to those six styles. This expanded understanding of evangelistic roles will assist us in making use of a variety of gifts and talents that can be used for various approaches to evangelism. Outreach which employs such multifaceted roles may better serve the needs of the whole person in various ways.

Also, it can be asserted that various types of human characters can contribute to making the Christian message alive, since, in terms of communication, ecological thinking concerns life in its entirety. The ecological vision this study seeks is, however, not entirely congruent with the principles and methods of the Contagious Witness program. The evangelistic model developed and implemented in most representative seeker sensitive church falls mostly under the category of personal evangelism. Nevertheless, this study recognizes the CW program as making a particular contribution to identifying and encouraging the diverse gifts and personalities of different people and their potential for evangelism in a number of ways.

Reciprocal Relations

The value of a relational approach has been stressed in new models of evangelism which focuses on Christian presence and lifestyle. Prior to delivering a prepared presentation of a gospel outline to the potential convert, relationship building is highlighted in importance. One instance of this case is found in the training program of CW curriculum. The training components are composed of twelve sequential programs ranging from instilling a vision of evangelism, embodying an authentic Christian life, to invitation to decision, and follow-up for discipleship.[224] In the middle of this training sequence, building and deepening relationships with non-Christian friends is highlighted in importance because the battle for winning souls "will be won or lost right here."[225] This call for deepening relationships with people should not be discounted on the basis of its indirect approach. Among the Christian community, it surely has contributed to an awakening to the value of real life and overcoming some of the event and action oriented notions concerning evangelism.

At this juncture, the nature of authentic relationships needs more careful deliberation. When developing relationships with non-Christians has an evangelistic purpose, there always arise questions of motivation which potentially reduce relationship building to a manipulative dimension. On this topic, two points need to be made. First, the building of relationship in evangelism must emerge out of a natural encounter with non-Christians rather than out of a contrived approach. Such a contingency would require Christians to engage in the public area of life not only for the sake of evangelism,

---

[224]Ibid., 161.
[225]Ibid., 163.

but more fundamentally for affirming the value of the Kingdom in every area of life. This point is underscored when we come to terms with the doctrine of Common Grace in the macrosystem of evangelism.

Secondly, Christians bear the mandate of hospitality to strangers. Hospitality can be understood as a pure act of service to others with love and respect. Throughout the Bible, the people of God have been encouraged to show hospitality (Exod 22:21; Lev19;34; Deut 10:18-19; Matt 8:20; Heb 13:2; 1 Pet 4:9). Practicing hospitality is possible in our current situation, simply by developing face-to-face relationships with neighbors and showing interest in the daily lives of others. Thus, it becomes important for Christians to locate themselves in open spaces where natural encounters with others are possible and which facilitate a communal sense in the midst of daily life.

Hospitality also involves receptivity, not just activity. It is different from serving a guest in a hotel room, which requires no personal relationship. "Receptivity means that I invite the other to 'be at home' with me. A home receives the imprint of one's personality: something of myself is infused into the way my home-space is constructed."[226] Thus, acts of hospitality affirm individual difference and particularity. The person who is hospitable and available should listen to the other in dialogue unlike the way one might behave when engaging in acts of propaganda, manipulation and self-promotion.[227] Hospitality, understood in this way, offers a model for developing more reciprocal relationships.

Christine Pohl distinguishes hospitable acts from service-oriented acts which tend to objectify the person. While the former focuses on the whole person, the latter on the particular needs in problem. She argues, "Effective treatment does not allow one to be receptive to the whole person of the client; only those traits that are deemed relevant to the task at hand can be attended to."[228] Instead, she strongly affirms the practice of hospitality in recovering the genuineness of relationship. "A distinctive feature of many contemporary advocates of hospitality rather than service is their rejection of bureaucratic styles of helping. They stress minimal scrutiny and focus instead on respect and friendship."[229] Thus the genuine practice of hospitality allows for a reciprocal relationship between host and guest.

It may well be that the enormous appeal of the Alpha course among non-Christians stems at least in part from its non-threatening approach to and respect for interactive conversation. It is reported that "Alpha's openness to

---

[226]Neil Pembroke, *The Art of Listening: Dialogue, Shame, and Pastoral Care* (Grand Rapids: Eerdmans, 2002), 21.

[227]Ibid., 45.

[228]Christine D. Pohl, *Making Room: Recovering Hospitality as a Christian Tradition* (Grand Rapids: Eerdmans, 1999), 162.

[229]Ibid., 163

questions allows people to experience learning about the Christian faith in a way that is not threatening"[230] despite its formularized curriculum.

Reciprocity also requires sharing life together in all of its aspects. Relationship, thus, should not be reduced to its instrumental value. To seek reciprocity in building up relationships will, in fact, aid the evangelistic advocate in discerning the needs and situation of the potential convert and will help suggest ideas for a relevant approach as well. Emphasis on reciprocal relationship and joint activities necessitates the establishment of wider indirect settings for evangelism.

Summary

Microsystem in evangelism deals with the immediate settings for intentional evangelism. Despite the fact that microsystem concerns direct ways of evangelism, an overarching ecological insight provides a deeper perspective from which to probe the rich diversity of evangelistic channels and roles, and to inquire into the nature of relationship. This is the first step an ecological approach enters into in order to move beyond the mechanistic and mathematic way of treating evangelistic communication. But an ecological approach to evangelism also engages in the larger inter-connecting settings.

Prior studies of evangelism have concentrated almost exclusively on planning programs, designing methods of presenting the gospel, and forming immediate settings that directly influence transformation of the potential convert often ignoring the interconnections between those settings and others in which the potential convert encounters in normal life. In the following discussion, it will be argued that the capacity of a particular evangelistic setting to generate and sustain ongoing intentional evangelistic activities will depend on relationships between that setting and others.

Mesosystem and Evangelism

A mesosystem is defined as "a set of interrelations between two or more settings in which the developing person becomes an active participant."[231] It is assumed in the mesosystem context that the establishment of linkage between settings will significantly enhance human development. Bronfenbrenner proposes several hypotheses (from his comprehensive research findings) about ecological transitions as well as the participation of a developing person within the interaction of different settings. In sum, the Bronfenbrenner repeatedly finds that there is a connection between the developing person's participation in different settings and the existence of a supportive link between settings.[232]

---

[230]Morgan, 38.
[231]Bronfenbrenner, *The Ecology*, 209.
[232]Ibid., 211-217.

The main premise with regard to mesosystem and evangelism arises as follows. The appeal of the Christian message will be enhanced to the extent to which all different outreach settings that potential converts may experience are tightly connected. Thus the rational content of the Christian message is not severed from other dimensions of Christian life. This mark of mesosystem invites the evangelistic communicator to consider the following aspects: (1) intracommunication linkage; (2) intercommunication linkage; and (3) a supportive relational network.

Intracommunication Setting: Integration

It has already been noted that multiple modes of communicative channels, verbally or nonverbally, affect one's reception of a certain message. Putting this communication insight in terms of religious education and evangelism, Babin brings up the concept of modulation. In this, he strongly opposes the notion that the audiovisual functions merely as an illustrative aid to written or verbal communication—which tends to appeal to the intellectual dimension of the human person. He means, by modulation, "a whole complex of vibrations varying in intensity and pitch, with special rhythms and tones of their own."[233] He goes on, further, to contend that the range of modulation should include everything presented to the human senses "as vibrations which can be seen, heard, or felt and which have a rhythm, intensity, or scope that nowadays can be increased electronically."[234] To Babin, the audiovisual aspect of communication accents and enlivens the experience of reality. One example of this modulation effect is the role of Pope John Paul II. Babin appraises the effective ministry of Pope John Paul II in terms of effectuating modulation.

(H)is gestures, voice, projection, and body language are all actor's modulations, which electronics exaggerate. . . . On his 1984 visit to Thailand, citizens of that country remarked, "It is impossible to understand how he can be so natural and smiling after so little rest and after enduring the heat in our country." It was not Pope John Paul II's words, but his modulation that led to so many conversions on that visit.[235]

Modulation can work as a corrective to disengaged communicative channels. It might be encouraged in order to widen modes of communication for an effective presentation of a given message. In addition, linkages between different communicative senses must be considered in significance, since harmonious interconnection can express the beauty of the message delivered.

---

[233]Babin, 80.
[234]Ibid.
[235]Ibid.

Interconnection or modulation between channels of communication was a key aspect of L'Abri ministry founded by Francis and Edith Schaeffer. In evangelistic terms, the ministry of L'Abri was an exemplary phenomenon in that it adopted a new way of reaching the intellectually frustrated and culturally confused. While there have been numerous approaches to understanding the thought and work of the Schaeffers in light of evangelical cultural apologetics, there are other vital aspects to the ministry of L'Abri which come to light if one takes a glimpse of the real life situations that have happened in L'Abri. It is generally understood, among evangelicals, that Schaeffer expanded the dimension of apologetics and encouraged evangelicals to engage in dialogue with modern art, pop culture, and secular philosophers.[236]

It may be inferred, nevertheless, from reading the letters and writings of Edith Schaeffer about the inner life of L'Abri that at the heart of Schaeffer's provocative thoughts were living realities that were practiced by residents as well as demonstrated to the eyes of skeptics and seekers who visited L'Abri.

The defining feature of L'Abri is grounded on the fact that the Schaeffers, though they did significant works of apologetics, first of all, identified themselves as evangelists before Christian philosophers or critics of secular culture.[237] The evangelistic strategy of L'Abri is a community-based intellectual challenge to secular worldviews and distorted notions of truth. The shape of community pursued in L'Abri was imbued with artistic beauty, warmth of atmosphere, hospitality, and shared routines.[238] This exemplary Christian community was the footing upon which an intellectual quest of truth was encouraged and explored. The Schaeffers developed a pattern of meals, walks, and Sunday church services all geared toward providing an atmosphere that would stimulate conversation about philosophical and religious ideas. This integration gives flesh to the content of the message they attempted to deliver. Historian, Michael Hamilton describes the ministry of L'Abri in its blending of intellectual quest and hospitality.

> In this the Schaeffers were brilliant. For Edith, homemaking was high art, and she created an atmosphere that drew people in and invited them to relax. Francis was a superb and caring interlocutor who listened attentively, made

---

[236]Kevin G. Ford, *Jesus for a New Generation: Putting the Gospel in the Language of Xers* (Downers Grove, IL: IVP, 1995), 174 & 220. Here Ford contends that Schaeffer's method was propositional through logical argument. But he fails to portray the ministry of L'Abri in communal terms, but only through Schaeffer's books and lectures.

[237]Francis A. Schaeffer, *The Complete Works of Francis A. Schaeffer: A Christian Worldview*, Vol. I., (Westchester, IL: Crossway, 1983), 185.

[238]An account of life in L'Abri can be found in Edith Schaeffer, *The Tapestry: The Life and Times of Francis and Edith Schaeffer* (Waco, TX: Word Books, 1981). Especially, see chapter 18.

guests feel important, and spoke with earnest confidence of Christianity's ability to solve the human dilemma. . . . A number of students converted to Christianity as a result of these weekends, and a few volunteered to stay on to help with the growing workload.[239]

Along with intellectual honesty the hospitable atmosphere was the critical component that creates the ministerial circumstance of L'Abri. Describing how Christians can recover the beauty of life in the context of a home, Edith Schaeffer developed the notion of hidden art to show how ordinary areas of everyday life could be infused with creativity, beauty, and imagination. Schaeffer reveals many places where beautiful and artistic expression can be found in the context of normal family life. As she explains, "to develop hidden art will also take time and energy."[240] The artistic value of minor areas such as interior decoration, floral design, food, serving, letter-writing, clothing, and sketching is enhanced when those areas are interweaved into tapestry.

Schaeffer sees every area of daily routine in its relation to art. Moreover, the shape of daily living is, itself an art form constituting an "environment" in which others whom we encounter live. She describes this concept,

> After all we are an art form. I do not mean that we produce at consciously now, but I mean we are an art form, whether we think it or not, and whether we do anything about it or not. We are an environment, each one of us. We are an *environment* for the other people with whom we live, the people with whom we work, the people with whom we communicate.[241]

Based on this it is clear that the best environment for evangelism arises out of integration between various activities. Integration will be helpful towards harmonizing the factors of microsystem into a coherent message. The concept of "integration" will function as the key to linking those multi-senses in the life of a Christian family, which Schaeffer believes, is the optimum locus, to demonstrate the reality of Christianity. She describes true integration as having "spiritual communication and fellowship together, discussing and discovering new thoughts and ideas by sharing their trends of thought, or thinking out loud and having some kind of creative activities or recreations together."[242] Integration undergirds the development of L'Abri ministry and implies a wider dimension including the intermingling of members of various races, nationalities, generations, education levels, and occupations. Sensitivity to integration plays a role in combining work, teaching, and life in harmonious oneness.

---

239 Michael S. Hamilton, "The Dissatisfaction of Francis Schaeffer," *Christianity Today* (March 3, 1997), 25.

[240]Edith Schaeffer, *The Hidden Art of Homemaking: Creative Ideas for Enriching Everyday Life* (Wheaton, Il: Tyndale House, 1971), 32.

[241]Ibid., 208.

[242]Ibid., 200.

In addition, we have seen how diverse roles among Christian advocates are brought into the scene when witnessing to the gospel. The mesosystem focus on integration for evangelism may play a critical role in promoting cooperation among such diverse types, allowing the message to be delivered more effectively through their concerted effort.

In addition, potential converts at L'Abri were encouraged to ask honest and intellectual questions while participating in the truthful life of L'Abri. This allows for them to be active and reciprocal subjects in their own spiritual journey. These two aspects are congruent with the mesosystem, which refers to a set of interrelations between two or more settings in which the developing person becomes an active participant.

The connection between the embodied life and the gospel message is particularly important for our desire to make evangelism come alive, since both embark upon human desire at a deeper level. It may well be that artistic embodiment through normal life along with elaborate artifacts is the other side of the equation in expressing the Christian truth. If this consistency between the spiritual aspect and the artistic value in normal life is in deficiency, the Christian message is not appealing as much as when both are integrated.

Intercommunication Setting: Blending of Settings

Mesosystem analysis emphasizes the interconnection between communicative settings as well as integration within a communicative paradigm. If a message is to be conveyed with a wide variety of communicative channels such as word, music, arts, atmosphere, and hospitality, those channels need to be harmonized in such a way as to make the message vivid. Equally, the synchronized message will be more enhanced by being blended with cultural manifestations from the religious advocates. Previously, this study noted the importance of consistency and coherence between different modes of direct influential communication as in the ministry of Schaeffers. In much the same vein, the church's action and attitudes in areas beyond evangelistic activities are also to be considered in light of mesosystem principle, which sees connection between settings.

One example is the various ways of relating the religious dimension with social service. Sider and his colleagues describe the four types of church's reaction in constructing the relationship between evangelism and social ministry.[243]

The first type is the church where explicit evangelism is not a part of its outreach mission. This type of church may be committed to the ministry of satisfying the physical and social needs of the community, but not concerned with nurturing faith and promoting belief in the gospel. "Often this type of church's approach to social action is based on a theological understanding

---

[243]Subsequent discussion of the four types of relating evangelism and social action is quoted in Sider and *et al*, 110-113.

that equates evangelism with doing good works."[244] This understanding of evangelism does not take into account evangelism as communicating the core message of Christianity and inviting people into discipleship. Also, this perspective may overlook the foundational motivation of personal conversion for social change or stem from previous negative experiences with forceful and insensitive evangelism.

In the second type of church "evangelism is valued and practiced but not in the context of social ministry."[245] This type of church is aware of both spiritual and social needs, but in a dualistic way. Hence the program of evangelism does not engage the social dimension as it comes into contact with others outside the church just as the church's social ministry does not touch the evangelistic need for nurturing faith and assisting one's spiritual pilgrimage. Churches of this type may be actively involved in charity ministries toward those who are not within their surrounding community or are from a different socioeconomic class, but may practice evangelism only toward those within their local community.[246] Thus, while they can be committed to both areas of social ministry and evangelism, the normal life of their congregation may not be affected by a Christian conception of the whole person.

The third type of church is convinced that evangelism and social ministry are integrated in "an inseparable but indistinguishable way."[247] As pointed out earlier, the ecological vision of humanity looks at the fabric of human nature to be composed of a variety of physical, spiritual, moral, relational, and cultural dimensions. Likewise, this perspective strives to blend evangelism and social ministry in a mutually enhancing way. This type of approach is most commensurate with the holistic model that integrates the two seemingly different dimensions. While repudiating an exclusionary set of conditions for participation in religious activities, this integrative approach strives to create the opportunity for the beneficiaries of social ministry to learn about Christian faith.

This type is not entirely free of potential risks as it relates to social and spiritual values. A church of this type may run the risk of reducing "social ministry to a mere tool of evangelism."[248] Accordingly, the matter of motivation for social ministry needs to be examined to promote this model. In addition, "holistic churches that emphasize informal, relational evangelism should check whether the gospel message is actually being communicated."[249]

The fourth type of church regards evangelism as a solution to social needs. Sider and his colleagues state, "This type of church cares about healing social ills, but evangelism and discipleship are essentially the only vehicles for

---

[244] Ibid., 110.
[245] Ibid.
[246] Ibid., 111.
[247] Ibid.
[248] Ibid., 113-114.
[249] Ibid., 114.

outreach."[250] This supposition is characterized by a strong belief that reliable and lasting social transformation can come only from personal conversion and spiritual change. Churches of this type may engage in charity activities in some ways, but do not attempt to take into account the underlying problems that bring up the apparent social and personal miseries. This approach also overlooks the ecological insight that "our social environment has a profound effect on us."[251]

Describing and assessing the four types of relationship between social ministry and evangelism, Sider and others illustrate one case of holistic ministry in action from their research on churches in the metropolitan area of Philadelphia. They present Christian Stronghold Baptist Church as an exemplary church of a type three. This church is committed and effective in supplying people with various needs from food distribution to educational assistance. The church also incorporates service to the physical needs into the larger paradigm of evangelistic encounter. In order to obtain a clear grasp of this blended endeavor, a couple of cases need to be quoted.

In a program that helps new home owners obtain a mortgage, recipients hear about God's plan for their lives as part of the process of financial counseling. Counselors encourage new home owners to give God the credit for this life-changing blessing. At church-sponsored health fairs, doctors integrate spiritual and medical advice, telling hypertension patients not only about exercise and proper nutrition but also "that your body is the temple of the Holy Spirit and that you have a responsibility to be a steward of it."[252]

It is clearly evident from Sider's research team that evangelism and social ministry can be combined in the whole process of conversion and discipleship. It is expected in the context of the church that as members grow spiritually, they are more committed to service to the outside community. On the basis of this consistent interconnection between evangelism and social ministry, Christian Stronghold is able to experience the following noteworthy outcome in engaging its members in integrative and holistic ministry.

> According to our member survey, 90 percent of respondents said they often or sometimes talked about their Christian beliefs or testimony with non-Christians in the last year, and 70 percent invited people to church. And 82 percent of respondents said they helped lead someone to Christ! Christian Stronghold members are equally committed to demonstrating God's love with caring actions in their daily lives: 95 percent of respondents reported providing someone in need with food, clothing, or money in the last year; 83 percent helped someone find a job; and 82 percent took care of someone who was sick or handicapped. . . . Average adult Sunday morning attendance is about seventeen hundred-and roughly half of these people had never belonged to a church before Christian Stronghold.[253]

---

[250]Ibid.
[251]Ibid., 114.
[252]Ibid., 121.
[253]Ibid., 125-126.

The statistics above are not quoted to demonstrate the potential of holistic ministry for numerical growth of the church. The result of holistic ministry can only be proven on a long term basis. In spite of this caveat, it is clear that some combination of evangelism and social ministry can be a significant contributor to the full-dimensional growth of the local church and individual Christians. Such linkages among the church's outreach activities may help those outside the church experience the integrity of the message the church tries to communicate. When this happens, the developmental potential enhances in terms of mesosystem which emphasizes well-linked relations between settings.

Supportive Link of Spaces

Mesosystem also refers to second-order social networks involving intermediate links that can encourage the growth of mutual trust, positive orientation, goal consensus, and affective relations.[254] With regards to this supportive link, we may be able to surmise that personal support of potential converts by existing church members is a crucial factor in leading and incorporating them into the church structure. As mentioned earlier, microsystem includes all the present factors affecting the developing person. The range of microsystem factors can be diverse to the extent of including physical features. In light of an enhanced view of communication, it is permissible to broaden the spectrum of microsystem communication channels to include music, atmosphere, and image.

As evidenced in commercial atmospherics, space also speaks and affects our behavior and thought. The visual space of the church can imply and deliver a certain message in a similar way to the Christian homes of the early church which used decoration as a ground for evangelism. The language of space had been taken up by sociologist Edward Hall several decades ago. On the basis of understanding culture as communication, Hall argues that "the flow and shift of distance between people as they interact with each other is part and parcel of the communication process."[255] The meaning different spaces carry can vary according to culture. Distance and spatial sense can be a grid by which human beings distinguish themselves from and interact with others as they search for community. Based on the assumption of spatial communication and its anthropological implications, Hall lays claim to "proxemics" that addresses human patterns of participation in different spaces.

He asserts the following four distances that, in general, relate to the human person: intimate distance (six to eighteen inches), personal distance (one and a half to four feet), social distance (four to twelve feet), public distance (twelve to twenty-five feet or more). Each of these spaces can be fur-

---

[254]Bronfenbrenner, *The Ecology*, 216.
[255]Edward Hall, *The Silent Language* (Garden City, NY: Doubleday & Company, 1959), 208.

ther divided into close phase and far phase.[256] Human action can be enacted differently in dynamic response to different spaces and is regularly done so. Nevertheless, human perception of space has not been accorded due attention by social scientists. Hall suggests that this tendency to overlook the significance of spatial components which affect human behavior and thought may stem from two mistaken notions. One is that there is a single and identifiable cause to our actions. And the second is that the human boundary begins and ends with the physical skin.[257]

Building on Hall's proxemics for human action and perception, Joseph Myers emphasizes the need to widen our sense of community to include spatial factors in order to meet the real human craving for connection. He issues a warning against an over-emphasis on small groups (which can be categorized just by social or personal space) to create community. He proposes that each of these four spaces retains potential for creating community in different modes and this combination of four spaces will assist us in grasping the variety of communal settings.[258]

Among Christians, the term community has emerged as the most significant vehicle for exploring and establishing the body of Christ. As a means to evangelism, the rediscovery of the communal nature of witness and service has been deemed critically important. The efficacy of the small group structure has been emphasized as has the evangelistic value of public worship. However, as demonstrated in the previous chapter, an ecological perspective encourages us to consider the fact that human transformation occurs mostly in a developmental context. It may be too much to expect that the person on a spiritual journey skip to personal or intimate belonging without first going through the stage of public or social belonging.

Human participation in the community may also take time and energy. In this sense, the perspective of looking at all spaces equally becomes significant. Myers asserts, "Healthy community . . . is achieved when we hold harmonious connections within all four spaces."[259] He further argues, "A healthy strategy for those working to build community entails allowing people to grow significant relationships in all four spaces."[260] In terms of evangelism, the pursuit of harmony between those spaces should be considered as we think of gradual development of the human person in a spiritual sense.

These four spaces provide an outlet toward which churches can direct their evangelistic efforts. It may not be the case that any particular space excludes others in its effectiveness of communicating the gospel, yet at the

---

[256]Edward Hall, *The Hidden Dimension* (Garden City, NY: Doubleday & Company, 1966), 111-117.
[257]Ibid., 199.
[258]Joseph R. Myers, *The Search to Belong: Rethinking Intimacy, Community, and Small Groups* (Grand Rapids: Zondervan, 2003).
[259]Ibid., 51.
[260]Ibid., 52.

same time it may be true that there is a space more suitable for the particular needs of a given generation. Nonetheless, I would argue that each space has implications for approaching people evangelistically. The key lies in fostering a constructive interplay between the four spaces, while still maintaining a due regard for the separate importance of each.

Summary

The contour of mesosystem components with regard to evangelism has accompanied a repeated emphasis on integration or harmony as expressions of interconnection between settings--especially communicative settings in a larger sense. If we refer to theory of rhetoric, we see that harmonious integration makes a contribution towards making the message vivid and appealing . Rhetorical theory assumes that the most effective human communication (speech in particular) forms a triadic structure: logos, pathos, and ethos.[261] While the logos has to do with truth claims and pathos concerns emotional appeal, ethos constitutes an integral part of the argument's plausibility. Ethos is concerned with character or a way of life. Logos devoid of pathos and ethos is likely to lose its vitality of communication and fail to convey a holistic meaning . Pathos and ethos are cultivated and nurtured through a process which embodies the key elements of organic Christian life. All of these are ways of bearing witness, and the impact of words, emotions, and deeds together makes for a stronger witness than either one separately. In this regard, the Christian community is where the advocates' ethos and pathos as well as logos are created, developed, and embodied.

Mesosystem in evangelism focuses on the holistic quality by refusing to disengage the presentation of the gospel from the living out of the gospel. Holistic interation between various ministries of outreach is central to making the Christian message alive. However, an ecological approach moves us beyond such the holistic integration of immediate concerns to the seemingly remote settings that do not directly impinge upon potential converts, but influence people or structures that later affect the practice of evangelism.

Exosystem and Evangelism

Evangelistic synergy is put into use when ministry areas of the church encompass aspects that relate to basic human needs and desires. Those areas may not have to do directly with evangelistic activities and may not be explicitly fueled by evangelistic intentions. Through various channels, though, the church's commitment to addressing human needs contributes to enriching evangelism. This attention to outside influences is defined as exosystem in the ecological understanding of human development. With

---

[261]David S. Cunningham, *Faithful Persuasion: In Aid of a Rhetoric of Christian Theology* (Notre Dame, IN: University of Notre Dame Press, 1990), 39ff.

regard to the importance of intermediate links between ecological settings both in meso- and exosystems, Bronfenbrenner summarizes the following corollary hypothesis.

The developmental potential of a setting is enhanced to the extent that there exist direct and indirect links to power settings thorough which participants in the original setting can influence allocation of resources and the making of decisions that are responsive to the needs of the developing person and the efforts of those who act in his behalf.[262]

The evangelistic factors from an exosystem perspective do not include intentional activities that relate to the practice of witness to the gospel. They were not specifically designed for their evangelistic effect, though it may be the case that every aspect of the Christian community is interrelated to some degree with each other. In addition, the exosystem quality makes clear that human development, whether intellectual, emotional, or spiritual, should not be treated as a linear paradigm, but rather analyzed in terms of interconnected systems in an ecological context.

It may well be that this exosystem component is applicable to the plausibility structure that surrounds the developing person. "The plausibility structure is very simply a social structure which manifests the worldview of people."[263] This means that a certain life value "can only make sense ... in the expression of a social group that lives out, symbolizes and converses with that life world in ways that make it seem objectively and subjectively real."[264] Although the plausibility structure does not bring a certain message to the developing person in a direct way, it creates an external environment in which the person is obliquely influenced. Since ecological systems allows for a wider perception of the mode in which evangelism takes place, the notion of plausibility structure needs to be taken into account when we come to terms with a variety of evangelistic dimensions. As for evangelism, the plausibility structure can be described as the deeper social reality that the Christian value is potentially expressed in such a way that it fosters sharing the message of the gospel. Thus, the evangelistic capacity of the Christian message hinges upon the plausibility structure that the Christian community shapes in the larger society.

The plausibility structure is one that can be highlighted in terms of exosystem and evangelism. The life of the church in public realm is an important vehicle to carry its particular message, because "the firmer the plausibility

---

[262]Bronfenbrenner, *The Ecology*, 256.

[263]Dennis Hollinger, "The Church as Apologetic" in *Christian Apologetics in the Postmodern World* ed. Timothy R. Phillips & Dennis L. Okholm (Downers Grove, IL: InterVarsity Press, 1995), 186.

[264]Ibid.

structure, the firmer the view of reality on which that structure is built."[265] However, the plausibility structure does not merely have to do with the public realm outside the church, but also includes the inner structure of the church, where it can motivate Christians to further engage in evangelistic activities, even though the structure itself is not designed for intentional evangelism.

In order to explore the variables within the exosystem that relate to evangelism, we turn our attention to the notion of power settings. The ensuing paragraphs will expand on the notion of power settings (or plausible structure) in terms of evangelism as perceived in the light of exosystem. Three representative components of power settings, that may influence potential converts, are the social structure of the church, the physical aspect of the church, and the spiritual nurturing system of the church. The former two represent the external structure outside the church, while the latter addresses the internal structure of the church, although both do not have to do directly with explicit evangelistic purpose.

Social Structure

As mentioned in chapter three, Stark and Finke's emphasis on the significance of social attachment for religious conversion, (despite its failure to notice multiple components that accompanies religious transition), sheds some important light upon the way people are affiliated with religious organizations. First of all, Stark and Finke challenge the notion that it is rational choice with which causes the human person to enter into a new religious affiliation. Rather, they note that in, general, people choose a particular affiliation guided by their preferences and tastes.[266] In a similar way, Stark and Finke make a case that rational choice is often a matter of utility as well as a matter of taste or preferences. In so doing, they connect the notion of exchange (that fundamentally drives human action) and choice with the mathematics of pursuing the interest.

From carefully-researched data about shifting affiliation across religious traditions, Stark and Finke assert that social networks make religious beliefs plausible and "new social networks also reward people for converting."[267] Consequently, conversion is not understood primarily about seeking truth and doctrine but about "bringing one's religious behavior into alignment with that of one's friends and family members."[268]

This observation about religious change suggests that in understanding conversion, we ought to beware the overemphasis on the cognitive factors that bring about transformation. Rather "conversion proceeds along social

---

[265]Ibid., 186.
[266]Stark and Finke, 38.
[267]Ibid., 117.
[268]Ibid.

networks formed by interpersonal attachments."²⁶⁹ In another study of the rise of the early Christianity, Stark focuses on the public significance of the early Christian church in the Roman Empire. Although it started as a minor religion on marginalized areas, Christianity became the dominant religious force within a few centuries. Stark notes the public influence that the early church exerted such as extending communal care during plagues and famine, experiencing higher rate of fertility than the general population, and an elevated status for women that which served to draw women to Christian community. These social factors that the early church brought into the public realm were conducive to the growth of Christianity in the Roman times.²⁷⁰

The remarkable success of the Celtic mission was associated with the appeal of the monastic life. Rather than replicating the organizational structure of the contemporary Roman system, Celtic evangelists based their ministry upon monasteries which could be understood as community life. Monasticism made an enormous appeal among the Celts because the Celtic people were tied into the structures of kinship and clientage and there were no social organizations like provinces and fixed boundaries.²⁷¹ The monastic life was capable of accommodating itself to those structures, "because in an insecure and often violent world monastic communities were havens of security."²⁷²

Stark and Finke propose that "in making religious choices, people will attempt to conserve their social capital,"²⁷³ which consists of interpersonal networks. Thus religious reaffiliation tends to take place when the potential converts are overwhelmed by other religious institutions which offer other forms of social capital. Stark and Finke's analysis of religious conversion makes sense even within a cross-cultural setting,

A survey of Korean American immigrants' attitudes toward the church shows a marked difference from those of Koreans in Korea. One of the questions is, "how do you view the role of the church in the Korean American community?" The most common response among church goers (85 out of 202) was that "the immigrant church contributes to the development of the Korean American community," whereas non-church goers perceived this choice as fourth among six answers (including "others.")²⁷⁴ Contrariwise, a significant number of Koreans in Korea are more suspicious that Korean churches can play a positive role in developing the Korean society. A survey conducted in Korea indicates that Protestantism is seen by the majority of non-believers

---

²⁶⁹Ibid., 118.

²⁷⁰Rodney Stark, *The Rise of Christianity: How the Obscure, Marginal Jesus Movement Became the Dominant Religious Force in the Western World in a Few Centuries* (Princeton, NJ: HarperCollins, 1997), 128.

²⁷¹Fletcher, 90.

²⁷²Ibid., 91

²⁷³Stark and Finke, 119.

²⁷⁴"The Potentials of the Korean American Churches for Social Service and Guiding Young Generation," *Korea Times Daily*, 12 November 2004, 14 (A).

as an out-of-date religion with no favorable stance among the populace.[275] This discrepancy can be explained in part by reference to conversion as religious re-affiliation in pursuit of social capital. The immigrant context is one where the existing social and religious capital are disrupted to the point that people are inclined to seek new sources of social network that can favorably support their settlement in a new setting. In a new situation where churches are a major source of social life, people tend to be more attracted to the role of churches.

This account of conversion as adjusting religious choice to coincide with a particular life situation, of course, lacks consideration of the other ecological variables. It does offer, however, one aspect of understanding how people shift their religious affiliation which can aid Christian advocates in understanding how social structures can play a role in creating a plausible environment for the acceptance of the Christian faith.

One strategic case of this aspect of socialization is the promotion of evangelism for children. If spiritual development is construed as an adult phenomenon because conversion requires conscious choice and decision, attempts to convert children need to be understood in a different paradigm from decision-based evangelism. This does not mean that children are incapable of deciding for themselves. While the Evangelical tradition emphasizes the personal decision aspect of conversion (which is more generally applicable to adulthood), socialization as a conversion process is better suited for children.

It is reported that evangelism has been most effective among children.[276] This claim does not encompass the conversion cases of children in the present, but rather traces the mode of the surveyed adults' initial commitment to Christianity by age. It indicates that two out of three born again Christians embraced Christ before their 18th birthday. One out of eight born again people (13%) made their commitment to Christ while 18 to 21 years old. In addition, half of Christians made their profession of faith in their parents' guidance. It is also noted that the later the decision age is, the more it is likely to be led by friends or other variables such as media and events. Thus the report concludes that "people who became Christian before their teen years are more likely than those who are converted when older to remain absolutely committed to Christianity."[277]

---

[275]Gallup Korea, *Church Activities and Religious Consciousness of Korean Protestants* (Seoul: Tyrannus, 1999), 41. Negative impressions concerning Protestantism far surpasses those concerning Catholicism and Buddhism. 63 percent of those surveyed had Protestantism as past religion, while 16.8 percent for Catholicism and 20.2 percent for Buddhism.

[276]The subsequent paragraph is summarized with a direct quotation from the following source. George Barna, "Evangelism Is Most Effective Among Kids," *The Barna Updates*, 11 October 2004, <http://www.barna.org> (12 January 2005).

[277]Ibid.

While conscious conversion tends to be more of an adult experience, the socialization process (which has a profound influence upon conversion) begins at an early age. Evangelism to children is an optimal ministry to socialize people in the Christian paradigm of truth, morality, and life, because lifelong moral views are largely in place by adolescence.[278]

Building a plausibility structure in the community surrounding the church breaks important ground for evangelism and mission. The relationship between evangelism and social ministry has already been addressed under the heading of mesosystem. The value of social ministry is now reappraised with regard to building a plausibility structure in the community as a component of exosystem evangelism. In terms of ecological communication, social ministry itself bears some of the core messages of Christian truth such as sacrifice and loving service. When social ministry is engaged in as a direct expression of the love of Christ, it pertains to microsystem of evangelism. When this ministry is well aligned with other evangelistic ministries, it may be well that it has an impact on the mesosystem as well. On the other hand, the local church's engagement in a variety of forms of community development creates a supportive environment for the needy and creates a reputation of trust within the community. When this happens consistently over time, a new exosystem is formed, since exosystem concerns structure. This would, in turn, lead to an increase in social capital which, as we have seen, leads some people to be aligned with the church.

Physical Structure

In discussing the multi-dimensional nature of human communication, the role of the visual or the symbolic was noted. The visual is an important component in our experience of space and invites a response from participants in that space. Our experience of space itself is a sort of communicative process. The effect of carefully designed architecture can play a significant role in affecting peoples' feelings and persuading them to participate in the reality on which a structure is built.

There is another noteworthy insight into the use of space when we consider the physical feature of the church's evangelistic project. The New Urbanist movement and its rediscovery of the importance of public space in the making of community provide a fresh look at space adjacent to the local church. The importance of the space has been noted in church growth related literature as well. Wagner highlights the location of church in the strategy of church planting with a strong recommendation to conduct demographic and geographic research,[279] and Callahan broadens the concept of accessibility

---

[278]John W. Kennedy, "The 4-14 Window: New Push on Child Evangelism Targets the Crucial Early Years," *Christianity Today* (July 2004), 53.

[279]Peter Wagner, *Church Planting for a Greater Harvest: A comprehensive Guide* (Ventura, CA: Regal Books, 1990), 80-93.

and visibility by taking note of the shape of the church building, its location within the larger community, and its public relation strategy.[280]

Their insights into the space of the church are worth considering on a practical level. However, it is obvious that both works do not tackle the matter of quality of space with regards to urban life in particular. Their strategies are grounded on and developed from the suburban phenomenon which is particular to modern American society. Moreover, they do not grapple with the technological developments that have had a profound impact on contemporary urban and suburban structures. Emphasis on accessibility and visibility is largely dependent on a standpoint that takes automobile transportation and suburbia trend for granted for while failing to take note of the changed pattern of life this transportation trend has brought. This oversight has prevented them from noting the basic fact that suburbia disengages people from face-to-face relationships and threatens natural contact with neighbors.

Relocation to suburbia may disconnect the church from direct contact points with real life of people in the community, which would, in turn, divest the church of opportunities for Incarnation in the midst of the world into which it is called for witness. The matter of public space is reconsidered here again. Unlike its outer sacred architecture, the location of a church in its community does not appear to convey a particular message. However, the location of the church within the public space has potential to generate or inhibit communal activities among the neighborhood.

In fact, an integral part of Jesus' ministry is His Incarnation in the world of concrete space and time. Through embodied life and shared space, Jesus developed face-to-face contact with human persons. The literal meaning of Incarnational ministry implies that it must find its locus among neighbors and in everyday life activities. Thus the Incarnational principle highlights the importance of shared space in evangelistic communication.

For an example of using public space in evangelism, Eric Jacobsen assesses the success of Young Life group in reaching the younger generation with the message of the gospel. In a brief account of Young Life's activities, Jacobsen observes the pattern of Young Life outreach in a spatial sense. The effectiveness of Young Life outreach may be attributed to its choice of public space which allows its outreach members easily make contact with other young people outside the Christian community.[281]

From a practical perspective, the use of space is important in outreach to the public. Sharing space with the public resonates with the principle of Incarnation which communicates the stunning message that the divine being entered the mundane world, because "Incarnational ministry is much more

---

[280] Kennon L. Callahan, *Twelve Keys to an Effective Church: Strategic Planning for Mission* (New York: Harper San Francisco, 1983), 79-84.

[281] Eric O. Jacobsen, *Sidewalks in the Kingdom: New Urbanism and the Christian Faith* (Grand Rapids: Brazo, 2003), 82.

natural and comfortable in settings that have good public spaces."[282] Similarly, Michael Frost and Alan Hirsch articulate four characteristics of Incarnational missional churches: "proximity spaces, shared projects, commercial enterprises, and emerging indigenous faith communities."[283] Among those four, proximity spaces are "places or events where Christians and not-yet-Christians can interact meaningfully with each other."[284] In particular, Frost and Hirsch present cases of community-based business that develop commercial enterprises in a particular context with a view to embody the Christian presence in their midst.[285] The Incarnational model, understood this way, involves sending Christians into the midst of public life rather than to attract people into the fixed church spaces just as God condescended into a human form rather than remain distant from humanity. Some effective emerging, missional churches around the world are lunching their ministries in places like pubs, galleries, day cares, bookshops, and cafes where such intersecting of relationships can happen naturally.

The external location and public features of the church's physical structure becomes an important matter in helping the church to rediscover the centrality of community among Christians and to bear witness to it on behalf of others. It may be a challenge for evangelism that Christian communities are removed from the midst of society. This may bring Christians into fewer points of contact with the world. The Incarnational principle, thus, may cause us to reconsider the physical location of an evangelistic community. The emphasis on the physical structure can become a place of encounter between Christians and those outside the Christian circle in a public arena. Place of encounter itself is not a direct method of evangelism, but can assist Christian advocates in creating natural spaces to share the Christian message with outsiders.

Spiritual Structure

We now turn our focus from conditions on the outside to the inner life of the church. In this, we will consider some activities that do not directly have to do with evangelism, but still bear upon the church's witness in significant ways. Attention will be given to the nurturing system within the congregation and the leadership structure among numerous possible variables, since these two components are regularly brought to light in the literature of congregational evangelism.

---

[282]Ibid.

[283]Michael Frost and Alan Hirsch, *The Shaping of Things to Come: Innovation and Mission for the 21st-Century Church* (Peabody, MA: Hendrickson, 2003), 24. Frost and Hirsch illustrate the numerous cases of emerging missional churches that have tried to embody themselves in the shared spaces to bear witness to the Christian faith.

[284]Ibid.

[285]Ibid., 26.

Pastoral Care System

As seen in the previous pages, systems thinking explores the wider dimension of a structure in which a certain issue is situated rather than touching upon the symptom itself. By refocusing on the root problem within systems, one may be able to handle the relevant problem relationally. This principle applies equally to evangelism. Evangelism does not become successful by only focusing on the contents of evangelism such as evangelism training, sharing a vision for the unchurched and introducing new models. Systems thinking has helped us to see that of equal importance is the congregants' emotional and spiritual process.

One important area regarding exosystem is the matter of whether there is a supportive and nurturing group for the evangelistic advocates within the church. According to Hunter's observation, active lay ministry, which serves as a source of regular pastoral care to many congregants, gives an impetus to producing Christian advocates who share their faith and invite people to Christ. Regular pastoral care is an important producer of a people who share their faith. Most Christians who share their faith and invites others to Christ and the Church are themselves in regular spiritual conversation and prayer with a significant other who serves as their pastor. Most of the Christians who do not share and invite are not regularly pastured by anyone. . . . Most people in most churches do not receive regular pastoral care, and this is yet another cause of the stagnation of traditional churches.[286]

In addition, if evangelism in its diversified forms is to be understood as the responsibility for every believer, the existence of a spiritual support-system behind the evangelism is crucially important. Hunter reaches the conclusion (from a myriad of interviews with people in highly evangelistic churches) that "people who do engage in witness and inviting are very likely to be involved in a small group where people share their experiences and discuss the faith."[287] It can be asserted that the more congregants feel themselves cared, the more they become active in outreach witness.

The nurturing system, though not intentionally evangelistic, motivates and sustains evangelistic commitment among believers. Without the confidence of being fully supported, they would not be able to go out to share the gospel of Christ with others. Thus, an evangelistic exosystem refocuses our attention to a further structure of care system beyond stressing the evangelistic mandate and requiring the witness training program. The more people are cared for, the more they care for others in such a way that they can ex-

---

[286]George G. Hunter, *Church for the Unchurched* (Nashville: Abingdon, 1996), 120.
[287]Ibid., 115.

tend what they acquire through pastoral care to their interactions beyond the walls of the church.

Leadership Pattern

Leadership delegation to the laity also has an indirect bearing on reaching of the unchurched. If the burden of pastoral care is placed solely upon the senior pastor, it is likely to be carried out only at the time of crisis, not on regular basis. Dale Galloway, New Hope Church's senior pastor, hints that pastoral ministry should not be designed to reach and service the many needy, struggling, and dysfunctional people and families out there by targeting them alone. He argues that if the church directly focuses on and values certain ministry activities, "they will drain a church leader's energy and a church's finances, and many of them may never be in a position to prosper, pay their way, and support the expanded level of staff, facilities, and programming that it takes to serve more people like them, much less reach a city."[288]

Furthermore, when the senior pastor assumes all the duties of pastoral care, there will not be sufficient time for preaching and teaching, which are the primary duties of professional ministers. Most churches cannot afford enough professional staff to reach all congregants with pastoral care. After surveying the traits of churches that are effective in reaching the unchurched, Hunter makes the case that lay ministry has been the single greatest key to reaching the unchurched. In churches where lay ministry is encouraged, "the staff's key role is to 'lead and feed' the laity, thereby 'equipping the saints' for their ministries."[289]

It is evident that a strong presence of ongoing pastoral care by lay leaders contributes to the producing of disciples who willingly share their faith in the marketplace. As Hunter claims, "the correlation between the lay ministry and witness is very high, perhaps the highest of any of the correlations I have emphasized in this book, even higher than whether Christians have had evangelism training."[290]

Most ministry based evangelism is initiated and carried out by lay people who are adequately nurtured by the lay leaders or pastors in the local churches. Lay people are more often effective and authentic in discerning the felt needs of the unchurched seekers and what the surrounding community wants. There is, therefore, a deep connection between regular pastoral care and the production of lay witnesses who live in the midst of the real world. The evangelistic exosystem depends on this aspect.

---

[288]Ibid., 112.
[289]Hunter, *Church for the Unchurched*, 103.
[290]Ibid., 145.

Summary

To conclude, from exosystem perspective, we gain insights about the structures that lie behind our evangelistic efforts. Structures (whether social, physical, or spiritual) that surround the church, despite their not having an explicit evangelistic purpose, must be taken into account, because of their significant indirect bearing upon the church's evangelistic efforts. It is a commonly understood that "once a congregation loses its relationship to the community around it, it is only a matter of time before that church dies."[291] Social and physical structures serve as a foundation to facilitate evangelistic encounters with the unchurched, even if those structures do not directly articulate evangelistic values. Also, a solid spiritual structure within the congregation which promotes the morale of its members, though seemingly not related to evangelism, constitutes a larger environment out of which where the acts of evangelism naturally emerge. Any attention given to these structure are in tune with the exosystem which attends to the external settings that do not directly concern human development, but indirectly influential to it. These exosystems bring hardly any communicative message to potential converts. However, they play a significant role in reinforcing the more direct messages that are delivered in micro- and mesosystems, and for building stages for evangelistic communication to occur.

Macrosystem and Evangelism

Macrosystem refers to any sustained ideology which governs the people of a certain group or culture. The mindset (or core values) shared by group members also greatly affects human development of the subjects within the group. In regards to the macro factors that are correlated with evangelism, theological beliefs and congregational vision of evangelism can also be taken into account. As shown in related literature, this aspect has much to do with the effectiveness of evangelism.

With regard to the long term effects of evangelism, the congregational leaders' understanding and consideration of culture can make a difference. The churches that take into account the macrosystem elements of evangelism will generally attempt to be relevant to the culture of people in their community. Hunter asserts that "the leaders of those effective churches reaching to the unchurched all share a similar perspective: taking the local culture seriously."[292] Effective evangelism must be grounded in an understanding sensitive to the surrounding culture. Understanding the culture of the audience is foundational to developing the conceptual point of contact and constructing specific evangelistic plans.

---

[291]Text Sample, *U.S. Lifestyles and Mainline Churches: A Key to Reaching People in the 90's* (Louisville, KY: Westminster/John Knox Press, 1990), 26.
[292]Hunter, *Churches for the Unchurched*, 55.

In an example of this, William Dyrness focuses on exemplary American value systems and addresses the response of the Christian gospel to them. He probes three cultural values that shape the American way of life and thinking: pragmatism, optimism, and individualism.[293] These three value systems are deeply related to the historical and geographical characteristics of America, and have further affected the American understanding of the gospel as well as shaped the practices of Christian life. For example, Dyrness takes note of the American Dream as it is associated with the Puritan ideal of new land and a new level of life.[294] This Puritan conviction has engendered the notion of Americans as a chosen people with special privileges and divine hope for a holy nation. This conviction has permeated period of Revivalism in the 18th century and has a profound effect on our thinking even today. The Puritan's sense of expectation in the new land appeared to have more to do with American evangelicals' emphasis on the concept of being "born again" rather than on the biblically more frequent theme of following the way of Jesus.[295]

Understanding culture is significant to the shaping and planning of evangelism, especially in light of the fact that "the meaning of the gospel (like the meaning of anything) is communicated in many ways through a culture, not through language alone."[296] It gives a wider framework in which we can reconsider and design conceptual points of contact, worship styles, communicative modes of witness, and church structures that resonate with the social environment of contemporary people.

However, there is one important caution in responding to the cultural forms and issues. While we attempt to address the cultural issues, there also needs to be tension between being relevant to culture by offering a contrast to its core value and adapting the gospel to such values. Our attempts at cultural engagement should always be grounded in a theology, which serves to guide our interaction with cultural issues.

Instilling a Theological Vision of Evangelism

There is another equally significant aspect of macrosystem factors which relate to evangelism. The macrosystem perspective on evangelism deals with a theological vision of the evangelistic advocates and congregations, since macrosystem refers to ideological framework for human development. A theological vision of evangelism as presented by the church leaders can constitute a solid ground for further evangelistic action. In his comprehensive survey of the formerly unchurched, Rainer states that what makes distinguishable effective evangelistic church leaders is their clear articulation of a

---

[293]William Dyrness, *How Does America Hear the Gospel?* (Grand Rapids: Eerdmans, 1989), 29.

[294]The enduing paragraph is summarized from Ibid., 61-81.

[295]Ibid., 78.

[296]George G. Hunter, *Radical Outreach: The Recovery of Apostolic Ministry & Evangelism* (Nashville: Abingdon, 2003), 79.

purpose that a church must have. "A church must understand its purpose and the pastor must lead the church to carry that purpose."[297] This point is also noted in the contagious change process developed by the Willow Creek Community Church. Foundational to the Contagious Witness program is the modeling of and instilling evangelistic values. These are then followed by more strategic plans such as empowering and developing evangelistic team and brainstorming outreach ideas.[298] However, simply emphasizing an evangelistic burden is not sufficient to instill a theological vision of evangelism. Sharing with the congregation the theological importance of evangelism requires a more rounded understanding of essential doctrines.

It has been observed that churches with a strong belief system attract the unchurched in greater numbers.[299] This can be explained by the fact that a macrosystem concerns dominant values which govern those who are influential to the developing person. This wider perspective also points to the significance of theological doctrines with regard to evangelism. Central to the community and specifically individuals attempting to reach the unchurched are vital doctrines that relate to evangelism such as love of God and love of neighbor,[300] Incarnation, Common Grace, Trinity, and the like. Theology is very important in understanding the larger framework which encompasses evangelistic activities. Thus, well-founded and shared theologies function as a driving force that motivates and sustains the Christian community in their efforts to reach the unchurched.

As far as the integration of L'Abri ministry (as seen in mesosystem of evangelism is concerned), it can be asserted that this integration of communication activities is grounded on a belief in the Trinity who maintains the inner integration between the three divine persons.[301] Thus communication of the Trinity is an original source from which we can communicate the beauty of Christianity to others through many aspects of life. As we have seen in the prescriptive phase, the plural and relational attempt at communicating the gospel is more in tune with the doctrine of Trinity than any other doctrine. Hunter recognizes that the multisensory approach of Celtic evangelism was gleaned from the Trinitarian way of interconnection.

> The doctrine of the Trinity became the foundational paradigm for Celtic Christianity. The doctrine informed the people's piety as well as the theologians' theories. The understanding of God as a unity of three persons, bound togeth-

---

[297]Rainer, *Surprising Insights*, 65.
[298]Mittelberg, 92.
[299]Rainer, *Surprising Insights,* 168.
[300]Jones, 12. The author here contends that evangelism should be grounded in the love of God and neighbor, the greatest commandments which precede the evangelistic mandate to make disciples.
[301]Schaeffer, *The Hidden Art*, 204-205. Edith Schaeffer cites the capacity of Christian communication within the Trinity as the great merit upon which our approach to normal life can be integrated and harmonized.

er in love, became the Celtic model for the Christian community; the understanding of God as a family of three persons defined the Christian family. Celtic Christians lived their daily lives, from waking up to cleaning up, from working to retiring, aware of the presence, protection, and guidance of all three persons of the Trinity.[302]

Hunter also affirms that the Alpha course is informed by a Celtic Christian vision of the Trinity who is immanent among the lives of believers. He maintains that, in general, what a typical Alpha course offers includes hospitality, meal, worship, humor, conversation, imaginative expressions, and emotional intimacy, which reflects the quality of the Trinitarian interaction out of love and respect.[303]

Summary

Macrosystem is also bound up with the evangelistic activity of communication. Foundational to active evangelistic models is the organizing philosophy that governs every act that relates to communication. How we view culture has a bearing on the crafting of the message as well as the media to employ in the practice of evangelistic communication. More importantly, culture shapes our audience with whom we enter into a dialogue for evangelism. The necessity of a theology for evangelism as the macrosystem will serve as the foundation on which to build evangelistic strategies and models (micro-, meso-, and exo-systems). The theological vision that evangelistic communicators possess as a driving force will determine the degree to which they participate in the life of witness. Also, the content of underlying theology will assist us in exploiting and shaping the relevant messages.

Ecological insights bring us into a dialogue with another larger system that we have to take into account. Now we complete our survey of evangelistic articulation within ecological systems by turning to the temporal aspect.

Chronosystem and Evangelism

Chronosystem "involves the patterning of environmental events and transitions over the course of life, as well as through socio-historical circumstances."[304] Evangelism, from a chronosystem perspective, sets the evangelistic scrutiny of an audience into its historical setting and examines the development of different cohorts over time. If historical reflection concerning spiritual quests is to be carried out on macro level of chronosystem, an approach to one's conversion as a process can be categorized as micro level.

Process is a key component in understanding human development and can be defined as "the exchange of energy between organisms and their

---

[302]Hunter, *The Way of Celtic Evangelism*, 82.
[303]Ibid., 113-114.
[304]John W. Santrock, *Life-Span Development* (New York: McGraw-Hill, 2002), 44.

environment."[305] Process continuously places people in dialogue with relations, symbols, and environments as they pass through their life. A reflection upon process, thus, encourages us to pay attention to the complex variables that affect peoples' spiritual development. The notion of spiritual pilgrimage is firmly embedded in process evangelism and assumes that all people are on a search for God,[306] even though their shape of search is not explicitly Christian. Viewing evangelism in terms of spiritual pilgrimage is best analyzed from the standpoint of chronosystem, because the individual is influenced by historical incidents changes over time.

The task of evangelism, then, is to enter into a dialogue with the potential converts by interacting with their life stories and helping them discern that they are on a journey to find God, to discover where they are in that journey,[307] and eventually assist them in making the link between individual need and gospel solution.[308] This resonates with the systematization of faith stages that were critically assessed when we examined how evangelism has been affected by technological values. What we need to be wary of is an uncritical acceptance of the technological mindset rather than seeing only its usefulness to various aspects of ministry. Also, when we attempt to apply the concept of spiritual pilgrimage to potential converts, we need to note, "While it is true that spiritual pilgrimage is this neatly defined for some people, the search for God is much messier for most."[309] Thus, the three steps of spiritual search as quest, commitment, and formation as in Richard Peace's geography of spiritual pilgrimage need applied with respect for individual particularity, and not taken as a standardized mechanism. Thus, construing conversion as process and evangelism as spiritual pilgrimage allow us to take into account the transformation of the human person over the course of life rather than looking only to the immediate effects.

Chronosysem brings us into a dialogue with stories of people and culture as we attempt to approch them evangelistically. It indicates that human beings are conditioned and shaped historically in context. They are not to be treated in a vacuum. The spiritual cravings of people may take different forms during different historical periods. Thus, a chronosystem approach will help us to approach potential converts with more understanding and patience. In concert with this awareness, our evangelistic attempts need to begin with listening to stories and with learning the cultural needs historically formed.

---

[305]Phyllis Moen, "Introduction," in *Examining Lives in Context*, ed. Phyllis Moen (Washington, DC: American Psychological Association, 1995), 9.
[306]Peace, 310.
[307]Ibid.
[308]Ibid., 312
[309]Ibid.

A Narrative Application of Ecological Systems: *Hitsujigaoka* by Miura Ayako

Stories filter thought and experience and provide to others secondhand accounts about how the world and reality opperate. Constructing, telling, and comprehending stories involves the most basic human mental processes, and this mental processes in turn makes the gathering of meaning from story possible and universal.

Out of consideration for this reality, I present a story that can, I think, embrace the essential points of evangelism in light of ecological principle. The story is entitled *Hitsujigaoka*(menas *Sheep-Raising Hill*) and was written by a Japanese Christian novelist Miura Ayako.[310]

The novel begins in the context of a women's high school in the northern region of Japan. Naomi is a high school student and a pastor's kid. She is decent in manner and character, but feels uncomfortable with her rival classmate Teruko who seems more popular with friends and boys, but is indecent in the eyes of Naomi. Ironically, both women are in love at the same time with one man named Ryoichi. Ryoichi secretly enjoys the love triangle between Naomi and Kyoko. In the end Ryoichi marries Naomi, but their marriage life becomes unhappy, because Ryoichi turns out to be an alcoholic, violent, and unfaithful. It is not long before Naomi begins to hate her husband, and finally abandons him. Ryoichi is left alone and has nowhere to go. To make matters worse, Ryoichi is suffering from lung cancer which has come about as a result of his sloven life. Naomi's parents persuaded her to bring Ryoichi to their home. They repeatedly emphasizesd the power of forgiveness which is at the bedrock of love to both Naomi and Ryoichi. However, Naomi cannot accept him in her heart, so she does not show any interest in him.

Ryoichi, who becomes accustomed to living with Naomi's parents, gradually begins to change. On the wall of his room is Rouault's painting of Jesus on the cross. As Ryoichi stares at the painting, his heart is deeply touched. Although he does not yet go to church, Ryoichi is, at one point, determined to live faithfully to his wife and to stop drinking and smoking. Moreover, his health begins to recover over time.

One day Teruko, who now runs a tavern, secretly makes a call to entice Ryoichi. Ryoichi is not reluctant to go, but is determined to break off any ties with Teruko gently. So he visits her, but on the way back home falls on a snowy road and cannot get up due to a narcotic that Teruko put in Ryoichi's wine cup to retain him at her place. And he dies there.

When Naomi and her parents pack up Ryoichi belongings, they find a painting that Ryoichi drew. It is almost the same as the picture that hung on the wall in their house and that Ryoichi liked to look at. But there was one

---

[310]Miura Ayako, *Sheep-Raising Hill*, trans. Soyoung Kim (Seoul: Sulwoosa, 2001). Page references to the Korean version of this book in this section of the chapter are given parenthetically in the text.

striking difference. In this painting, Ryoichi is kneeling down under Jesus on the cross and Jesus is looking down at Ryoichi with mercy and forgiveness. Also, Jesus' blood streams down Ryoichi's cheeks!

This compelling story offers some important insights into how conversion takes place in ecological systems. Components of each system are spelled out below.

Microsystem

The microsystem components that turned Ryoichi to Christ include stories, image, and hospitality. How Ryoichi comes to Christ is consistent, then, with our discussions of ecological systems up to now.

Story

Even though Naomi's parents pastor a church, they neither enforced their belief upon Ryoichi nor preached the gospel outline. Instead they keep telling a story about forgiveness and love. In conversation with Ryoichi and Naomi, Goske (Naomi's father) narrates a stunning story about his own experience of forgiveness.

> There was one man twenty years ago. When he was married and his wife gave rise to a baby, he had a terrible affair. To make it worse, the partner was his wife's sister who was already married. Can you guess how his wife responded to them knowing the affair after she had the baby? She said that she was married to a man, not God. "Man is not perfect" said she.... In saying so, she forgave her husband as well as her sister who betrayed her. She was a Christian. Then the man came to realize how powerfully forgiveness changed people. Since then, he quit his job and went to a seminary to become a pastor. The baby died of a sickness, and the next one was Naomi (my translation: 231).

Listening to this story with surprise, Ryoichi and Naomi felt how fragile human life is. The story reminds Ryoichi of the meaning of forgiveness as given freely in Christ. This story within the story shows, once again, the appeal of stroytelling in evangelism. Parables and stories are the vehicles that were actively employed by Jesus and church leaders throughout history, possibly because they "will be more likely to excite curiosity than propositionally presented outlines of the gospel."[311]

---

[311] Frost and Hirsch, 101.

Image

Ryoichi was moved by looking at Jesus' picture on the cross. It was Rouault's *Christ on the Cross*. He shared with one of his friends the unexpected feeling that he had from the painting.

> Well, as I looked at Rouault's Christ, I all of sudden felt something was approaching me, even though I have never read the Bible. It may be something like agony? It seems like feeling that this Christ has something to say to me. It's strange because such feelings have never come over me when I looked at Rouault's paintings before.... It may be pain or symphathy. I felt a deep comnfort when I saw that Rouault's Christ. That is, the words like truth, goddnes, and beauty came up to me.... Then what can my art works appeal to people's hearts? (222-223)

Image is the most represenative form of symbol, even though the scope of symbol is far beyond just the visual. Paul Tillich describes symbol as pointing beyond itself to something else and inviting the viewer into its meaning and power.[312] The unique function of symbols (as compared to general images) is in their participatory power. Since the image of Christ resonates with the life of Ryoichi as he questions the meaning of the agony and sorrow of Christ on the cross, the art work comes to Ryoichi as an obvious symbol. The symbol does not stand in a neutral position, but rather invites the viewer to participate in the reality to which it points.

Babin also emphasizes that symbolic language evokes feeling and longings, while conceptual language leads simply to abstract knowledge.[313] The symbol, as a transformig agent, affects the whole person. Rouault's painting of jesus on the cross spoke to Ryoichi's heart.

Hospitality

As empahsized in the previous pages, Naomi's parents' way of relating to Ryoichi was a demonstration of hospitality. Naomi's parents did not condemn Ryoichi, even though they were aware that Ryoichi had told endless lies to Naomi and even violated her. Naomi began to disdain Ryoichi and struggled whether to abandon him. But her parents just accepted Ryoichi into their house as he was, a human being made in the image of God. Their hospitality was accompanied with warm conversations as well.

Mesosystem

As regards relation between immediate settings, I take note of the whole atmosphere, which carries a more integrative nuance than hospitality alone. Hospitality can be an intentional act with evangelistic purpose. Intentional

---

[312] Paul Tillich, *A Theology of Culture* (London: Oxford University Press, 1959), 52-53.
[313] Babin, 155.

evangelistic activities (whether explicit or implicit), are combined to create atmosphere. Thus atmosphere emerges out of an integration of various evangelistic activities rather than a singular acitvity in itself. When Ryoichi confided in his startling feelings about the painting of Christ as with the above quote, Teruko, while visiting him, made a cycnical remark. "It's because you are in a place like this. You must be vulnerable to this atmosphere!" (222)

She must have felt a different atmosphere as well! But for Ryoichi, it was unexpected moment that he had never encountered before. Sharing stories, warm hospitable acts, and a pictorial representation of the Christian faith work in sync to give rise to a distinctive atmosphere that is persuasive to him.

Second, we can observe, that the roles Naomi's parents played were consistent and interrelated. As hosts, they had to perform dual roles of pastors as well as parents in law. As pastors, they provide stories about Jesus' love and forgiveness. They continued to show their hospitality as parents in law on the other hand. Their caring heart was evident in linking both roles. This demonstrates a link between the evangelistic settings in which Ryoichi participates.

Exosystem

The personal experience Naomi's parents had with the forgiveness of Jesus affected their approach to Ryoichi and Naomi. I discern a kind of process evangelism in Ryoichi's story. Here we may notice the spiritual structure that shapes Naomi's parents presence in their influence over Ryoichi.

Furthermore, they ministered to Naomi in their unwavering acceptance of her, even though she disobeyed them in marring Ryoichi. Their treatment of Naomi does not directly have to do with Ryoichi's conversion. But it can be assumed that Ryoichi might be able to see the consistent, compelling power of acceptance with which he was also welcomed.

Welcoming Ryoichi in the care of a house setting as a physical structure holds significance in light of the discussion of exosystem. This setting naturally brings Naomi's parents into personal and intimate contact with Ryoichi in the entirety of his life. Ryoichi's conversion gradually and quietly took place in the context of the Christian family. In fact, the Christian family can be understood an integrating place that combines all aspects of ecological evangelism. The family can concurrently be an embodiement of personality, symbols, ordinariness, and hospitality. Mercedes Iannone describes the family as the cradle of the symbolic way,[314] because interpersonal relationship, symbolic interaction, and physical environment are all components of the family.

Recent memetic studies show that a primary vehicle in the spreading of belief is the familial context.[315] That is, a certain thought or belief spreads most readily in a familial atmosphere. The intimate structure helps the mes-

---

[314] Babin, 168ff.

[315] Aaron Lynch, *Thought Contagion: How Belief Spreads Through Society* (New York: Basic Books, 1996), 41ff.

sage infiltrate smoothly into the mind of others. The importance of family for the church is found in the need to make the church a home. The church should be a reflection of what the Christian family looks like rather than being seen as an institutional religious system.

Macrosystem

It is evident that love, forgiveness, and accpetance run through this story. It offers a compelling question, "On what grounds can we forgive others?" Similarly, acceptance of forgiveness is a mark of genuine conversion. At the funeral service, Goske delivered a striking eulogy telling that everyone, with no exceptions, cannot live without God's forgiveness.

> Is it true that we stand before God to ask for forgiveness on behalf of others, not to condemn them. Look at this picture Ryoichi drew! This shows hs is asking for forgiveness beneath the cross. . . . I hereby confess before God and people that I, my wife, and Naomi have been judging and condemning him in heart. He already repented and God forave him, though . . . . Since the human being cannot live a day without making a mistake, we are not able to survive unless we are forgiven by God. (286-287)

Human beings make a mistake, but God forgives. Forgiveness is a lucid mark of being a Christian. "To actually forgive in such a way that relationships are restored and a new culture of mutual care and regard come into existence requires restoration of the moral structure of personal relationship."[316] It is a theology of forgiveness that entrenched Naomi's family. Forgiveness became an organizing principle that directed every aspect of their normal life to restore the one son.

Chronosystem

Ryoichi stayed as a family member in the house of his parents-in-law for several months. Rather than urging him to decide for Christ at the moment, they simply shared their life with him. They also continuted to affirm every change that showed Ryoichi's transformation. Ryoichi's friend witnessed that gradual transformation. "Whenever I visited Ryoichi (in his parents-in-law's house), he was turning to be a person with a peaceful and transparent spirit." (255)

Process evangelism may be possible not as a goal-oriented mentality but rather with a person-oriented care. Naomi's parents saw a struggling soul deep inside within Ryoichi and strove to speak to his soul. Too often evangelism takes the form of a program or system, but ecological evangelism should be biotic and personalist addressing the needs of the soul.

---

[316]Anderson, *The Shape of Practical Theology* (Pasadena, CA: Fuller Theological Seminary Press, 1999), 250.

Trinitarian theology provides the ground for us to reflect on the interrelatedness of the triune God in His redemptive ministry. The essential components of ecological systems in the practice of evangelism are in accordance with the communicative markers of Trinitarian discourse. The ecological systems model affirms plurality, relationality, and materiality as in the fashion of Trinitarian communication. The microsystem advances plural communicative channels and roles, and reciprocal relationship. Plural communication also underlines the role of material senses in making the gospel understandable. In fact, the whole ecological system recognizes the fact that there are multiple factors that affect human transformation. The mesosystem focuses on integration and harmonious links between immediate channels of communication. This sheds more lights on the relational factor of communication. The exosystem furthers the importance of relational interconnection with external settings which have no bearing upon the direct mode of evangelistic communication. However, these settings do influence the shape of communication. The macrosystem helps us to see how our communicative activities are related with more cultural and theological values we share in common. This also highlights relationality. Lastly, the chronosystem stimulates us to be aware that all human transformation through evangelistic communication takes place in the wake of historical process. The chronosystem in evangelism, I think, can be a reflection of the economic Trinity, the way the triune Persons, Father, Son, and Spirit, have been working together in renewing the world in history.

As the triune persons refer to each other in an interrelated way so as to accomplish their redemptive work in history, ecological thinking always guides us in constantly referring to the larger environments that interconnect with organisms to elucidate the problem. The shape in which ecological systems operate may be shown in figure 1. The five systems, while each has its own unique sphere, also interface with each other, affecting the condition of each system.

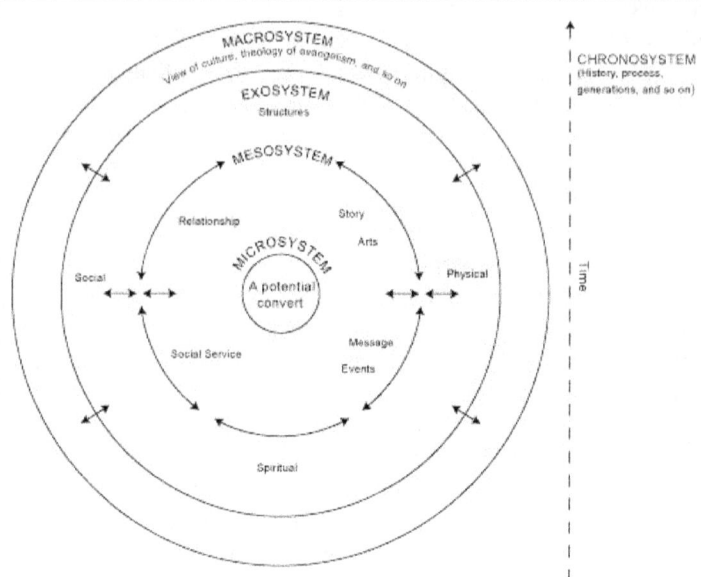

<Figure 1. Ecological Systems of Evangelism>

The microsystem covers all activities and ministries that directly reach people outside the church. This is the most typical area we have been familiar with in our efforts of evangelistic communication. Different microsystem components need to be integrated so as to effectively help people through transformational development. This is the central factor within the mesosystem. Thus the mesosystem concerns relation between microsystem components. While microsystem is enveloped by mesosystem, the former is also open to the impacts of the more external structures, exosystems, as seen in the figure. Likewise, while the exosystem covers micro- and mesosystems, it also intersects with macrosystem. Thus, the four systems are in an interrelated position as seen in the figure.

The chronosystem is outside the circles of systems, but affects the whole process of ecological systems.

The ecological systems model is a call to rethink how evangelistic communication actually takes place as well as how it is shaped in an interconnection of settings. This presents a critical issue as we engage a theological paradigm. Everything in the ecological approach may be seen as the work of the human spirit in its effort to understand and interpret the entire story of conversion and evangelism. But our preoccupation with ecological systems can also prevent us from inquiring into some of the more profound theological issues. It is out of a Trinitarian foundation that theology must "call the tune" if the ecological scope of evangelism is to be all-sufficient. This is the significant task we now turn to as we conclude this study.

Conclusion

The Trinitarian Consummation of Ecological Systems for Evangelism

We have now completed a tentative taxonomy of ecological systems and are in a position to theologically consider its missing link. In the foregoing discussion, we looked at the issue of how various settings can intersect in the practice of evangelistic communication. But theological consideration must be also be brought to bear on this ecological systems approach to conversion and evangelism. As I said of the ecological notion in chapter three, ecology itself needs to fit into a larger framework. We always must ask, "What can we affirm theologically about ecological systems of evangelism?" To look at ecological systems theologically will require further explorations of how evangelism is actually carried out.

We now turn back to the problems addressed in the Introduction. Simply emulating successful evangelism methodologies does not guarantee the same effect. Instead, what I have pursued throughout these chapters is a dialogue with a wider framework of thinking to which our actions are interrelated and then to consider systems which (directly or indirectly) influence our practice of evangelism.

While I suggest that we are able to gain much from ecological systems in understanding evangelism, I also want to affirm that they are under the controlling influence of the Trinitarian process. The relational nature of the world is a reflection of the Trinity.

Thus, I hereby advance a theologically more comprehensive concept, "a Trinitarian ecology for witness." It has often been argued that evangelism has been over-emphasized in the church, and that there hasn't been enough interest in renewing the community of Christ. This critical perspective may stem from a dualistic understanding of evangelism, which has inadvertently yielded a technological mode of communicating the gospel. In this mode, evangelism is understood only in terms of content rather than in terms of interrelatedness of content with context, and is disengaged from other activities of the church. This limited understanding of evangelism may contribute to a definition of evangelism which sees only individual acts or a separate ministry for growing the church. Evangelism is at the heart of the all of the church's activities. Abraham asserts, "evangelism enjoys a unique relation to the other ministries of the church.... It is not just one ministry alongside others: these latter ministries are all dependent on the ministry of evangelism."[317] First of all, evangelism is crucially significant because it seeks the most fundamental goal to transform a human person. Also, communicating the gospel necessarily involves the whole life of the church. All activities of the church and all aspects of Christian life bear impacts on the communicative effect of evangelism. When those activities are harmoniously interrelated, the effect of evangelistic communication would be enhanced. Evangelism is intended to reorient the life and direction of the church if it is to express the ecological web of Christian life. Only when ecological insights find their ultimate groundin the triune God who is creative and redemptive from beginning to end, a Christian community can rediscover the authentic value of evangelism and its organic relationship with other church activities in communicating the gospel.

Evangelism is about the whole system of the church. The assertion that evangelism should be relational, however, becomes a cliché unless we realize that evangelistic communication needs to recognize the relational web of all life systems in the life of a Christian community including its relationship with the larger society. Evangelism is interwoven with the fabric of person, society, and culture. With the aid of insights into the concepts of ecology and its systems approach to human development, evangelism can recapitulate Christian life as well as the community of Christians. There is an African saying, "it takes a whole village to raise a child." This ancient proverb conveys a central truth which accords with the gist of evangelism and is congruent with a Trinitarian ecology. "It takes a whole community to transform a person." I would suggest that we focus here on the concept of "whole" in a larger sense, including the triune God who has worked, is working, and will work toward consummation of humanity and all creation. We join this ecological community when we engage in the practice of evangelism.

---

[317] Abraham, 183.

Bibliography

Abraham, William J. *The Logic of Evangelism*. Grand Rapids: Eerdmans, 1989.

Anderson, Ray. *Christians Who Counsel: The Vocation of Holistic Therapy*. Grand Rapids: Zondervan, 1990.

Arthur, Diane. "The Importance of Body Language." *HR Focus* 72 (June 1995): 22-29.

Babin, Pierre and Mercedes Iannone. *The New Era in Religious Communication*. Minneapolis: Fortress, 1991.

Barna, George. "Evangelism Is Most Effective Among Kids." *The Barna Updates*, 11 October 2004. <http://www.barna.org> (12 January 2005).

_____. "Number of Unchurched Adults Has Nearly Doubled Since 1991." *The Barna Updates*, 4 May 2004. <http://www.barna.org> (12 January 2005).

Barth, Karl. *Church Dogmatic*. Vol. III:2. Translated by Harold Knight et al. Edinburgh: T&T Clark, 1960.

_____. *Church Dogmatics*. Vol. I:1. Translated by G. W. Bromiley. Edinburgh, : T&T Clark, 1975.

Bateson, Gregory. *Mind and Nature: A Necessary Unity*. New York: E. P. Dutton, 1979.

_____. *Steps to an Ecology of Mind: A Revolutionary Approach to Man's Understanding of Himself*. New York: Ballantine Books, 1974.

Begbie, Jeremy. *Voicing Creation's Praise: Towards A Theology of Art*. Edinburgh: T&T Clark, 1991.

Bendis, Debra. "ABCs of Faith." *Christian Century*, 9 March 2004, 22-27.

Borgmann, Albert. *Technology and the Character of Contemporary Life: A Philosophical Inquiry*. Chicago: University of Chicago Press, 1984.

Bradley, Ian. *The Celtic Way*. London: Darton, Longman and Todd, 1993.

Bronfenbrenner, Urie. "Ecological Systems Theory." in *Six Theories of Child Development: Revised Formulations and Current Issues* ed. Ross Vasta Vasta, 187-249. Greenwich, CN: JAI Press, 1989.

_____. *The Ecology of Human Development: Experiments by Nature and Design*. Cambridge: Harvard University Press, 1979.

Browning, Don S. *A Fundamental Practical Theology: Descriptive and Strategic Proposals*. Minneapolis: Fortress, 1991.

Callahan, Kennon L. *Twelve Keys to an Effective Church: Strategic Planning for Mission*. New York: Harper San Francisco, 1983.

Capra, Fritjof. *The Turning Point: Science, Society, and the Rising Culture*. New York: Bantam, 1982.

Capra, Fritjof and David Steindal-Rast with Thomas Matus. *Belonging to the

Universe: Explorations on the Frontiers of Science & Spirituality. New York: HarperCollins, 1991.

Conn, Walter. *Christian Conversion: A Developmental Interpretation of Autunomy and Surrender.* New York: Paulist Press, 1986.

Copleston, Frederick. *A History of Philosophy.* Vol. I. New York: Image Books, 1993

_____. *A History of Philosophy.* Vol. IV. New York: Image Books, 1994.

Costas, Orlando. "A Wholistic Concept of Church Growth." in *Exploring Church Growth,* ed. Wilbert Shenk, 95-107. Grand Rapids: Eerdmans, 1983.

Cunningham, David S. *Faithful Persuasion: In Aid of a Rhetoric of Christian Theology.* Notre Dame, IN: University of Notre Dame Press, 1990.

_____. *These Three Are One: The Practice of Trinitarian Theology.* Malden, MA: Blackwell, 1998.

Dawn, Marva J. *Reaching Out Without Dumbing Down: A theology of Worship for This Urgent Time.* Grand Rapids: Eerdmans, 1995.

_____. *Unfettered Hope: A Call to Faithful Living in an Affluent Society.* Louisville, KY: Westminster John Knox Press, 2003.

Dennis, Lane T., ed. Letters of Francis A. *Schaeffer: Spiritual Reality in the Personal Christian Life.* Westchester, IL: Crossway Books, 1985.

Dillenberger, John. *A Theology of Artistic Sensibilities: The Visual Arts and the Church.* New York: Crossroad, 1986.

Drane, John. *The McDonaldization of the Church: Consumer Culture and the Church's Future.* Macon, GA: Smyth & Helwys Publishing, 2001.

Dyrness, William A. *How Does America Hear the Gospel?* Grand Rapids: Eerdmans, 1989.

_____. *Visual Faith: Art. Theology, and Worship in Dialogue.* Grand Rapids: Bakers, 2001.

_____. "Art." in *The Complete Book of Everyday Christianity*, eds. Robert Banks and Paul Stevens, 45-48. Downers Grove, IL: InterVarsity Press, 1997.

Ellenberger, John D. "Evangelism Explosion and Communication: A Response." *Evangelical Missions* Quarterly 33 (July 1997): 304-306.

Ellul, Jacques. *The Humiliation of the Word.* Translated by Joyce M. Hanks. Grand Rapids: Eerdmans, 1985.

_____. *The Technological Society: A Penetrating Analysis of Our Technical Civilization and of the Effect of an Increasingly Standardized Culture on the Future of Man.* New York: Vintage Books, 1964.

Finnegan, Ruth. *Communicating: The Multiple Modes of Human Interconnection.* London & New York: Routledge, 2002.

Finney, John. *Recovering the Past: Celtic and Roman Mission.* London: Darton, Longman and Todd, 1996.

Ford, Kevin. G. *Jesus for a New Generation: Putting the Gospel in the Language of Xers.* Downers Grove, IL: InterVarsity Press, 1995.

Fore, William F. *Mythmakers: Gospel, Culture and the Media.* Cincinnati: Friendship Press, 1990.

Fowler, James. *Stages of Faith: The Psychology of Human Development and the Quest for Meaning.* New York: HarperCollins, 1981.

_____. *Becoming Adult, Becoming Christian: Adult Development & Christian Faith.* San Francisco: Jossey-Bass, 2000.

Friedman, Edwin. *Generation to Generation: Family Process in Church and Synagogue.* New York: Guilford, 1985.

Friesen, Duane. *Artists, Citizens, Philosophers: Seeking the Peace of the City.* Scottdale, PA: Harold Press, 2000.

Frost, Michael and Alan Hirsch. *The Shaping of Things to Come: Innovation and Mission for the 21st-Century Church.* Peabody, MA: Hendrickson, 2003.

Fuller, Robert C. *Ecology of Care: An Interdisciplinary Analysis of the Self and Moral Obligation.* Louisville, KY: Westminster/John Knox, 1992.

Gallup Korea. *Church Activities and Religious Consciousness of Korean Protestants.* Seoul: Tyrannus, 1999.

Gowan, Donald. *Theology in Exodus.* Louisville, KY: Westminster/John Knox Press, 1998.

Graham, William A. *Beyond the Written Word: Oral Aspects of Scripture in the history of Religion.* New York: Cambridge University Press, 1987.

Green, Michael. *Evangelism in the Early Church.* Grand Rapids: Eerdmans, 1997.

Grenz, Stanley. *The Social God and Relational Self: A Trinitarian Theology of the Image Dei.* Louisville: Westminster John Knox Press, 2001.

Groeschel, Benedict J. *Spiritual Passages: The Psychology of Spiritual Development.* New York: Crossroad, 1996.

Guder, Daryl L. "Incarnation and the Church's Evangelistic Mission." *International Review of Mission* 83, no. 330 (July 1994): 417-428.

Guiness, Os. *The Dust of Death: A Critique of the Establishment and the Counter Culture and a Proposal for a Third Way.* Downers Grove, IL: InterVarsity Press, 1973.

Gunton, Colin. *The One, The Three and The Many: God, Creation and the Culture of Modernity.* Cambridge, England: Cambridge University Press, 2002.

Hagberg, Janet and Robert Guelich, *The Critical Journey: Stages in the Life of Faith.* Dallas: Word, 1989.

Hall, Edward. *The Hidden Dimension.* Garden City, NY: Doubleday & Company, 1966.

_____. *The Silent Language.* Garden City, NY: Doubleday & Company, 1959.

Hamilton, Michael S. "The Dissatisfaction of Francis Schaeffer." *Christianity Today,* 3 March 1997, 22-30.

_____. "Willow Creek's Place in History." *Christianity Today,* 13 November 2000, 62-68.

Hawkins, O. S. "Reaching all the Nations: Lessons for the Next Stage of World Evangelism." *Evangelical Missions Quarterly* 33 (July 1997): 302-304.

Hawley, Amos H. *Human Ecology: A Theory of Community Structure.* New York: Ronald Press, 1950.

Heliminiak, Daniel A. *Spiritual Development: An Interdisciplinary Study.*

Chicago: Loyola University Press, 1987.

Hoekema, Anthony. *Created in God's Image.* Grand Rapids: Eerdmans, 1986.

Hollinger, Dennis. "The Church as Apologetic." In *Christian Apologetics in the Postmodern World*, ed. Timothy R. Phillips and Dennis L. Okholm, 182-193. Downers Grove, IL: InterVarsity Press, 1995.

Hunter, George G. *Church for the Unchurched.* Nashville: Abingdon, 1996.

_____. *The Celtic Way of Evangelism: How Christianity Can Reach the West...Again.* Nashville: Abingdon, 2002.

Jacobsen, Eric O. *Sidewalks in the Kingdom: New Urbanism and the Christian Faith.* Grand Rapids: Brazo, 2003.

Jeffrey, David L. *People of the Book: Christian Identity and Literary Culture.* Grand Rapids: Eerdmans, 1996.

Johnson, Todd. "Truth Decay: Rethinking Evangelism in the New Century." in *The Strange New World of the Gospel*, ed. Carl Braaten. Grand Rapids: Eerdmans, 1997.

Jones, Scott J. *The Evangelistic Love of God and Neighbor: A Theology of Witness & Discipleship.* Nashville: Abingdon, 2003.

Jüngel, Eberhard. *God as the Mystery of the World.* Translated by Darrel Guder. Grand Rapids: Eerdmans, 1983.

Kallenberg, Brad. *Ethics as Grammar: Changing the Postmodern Subject.* Notre Dame, IN: University of Notre Dame Press, 2001.

_____. *Live to Tell: Evangelism for a Postmodern Age.* Grand Rapids: Brazos, 2002.

Keel, Othmar. "Iconography and the Bible." in *The Anchor Bible Dictionary.* 6 vols. Edited by David Freedman. New York: Doubleday, 1992. 3: 358-374.

Kennedy, James. "Evangelism Explosion: 'Reaching All the Nations' and Its Impact On World Missions." *Evangelical Missions Quarterly* 33 (July 1997): 298-301

Kennedy, John W. "The 4-14 Window: New Push on Child Evangelism Targets the Crucial Early Years." *Christianity Today*, July 2004, 53.

Kimball, Dan. *The Emerging Church: Vintage Christianity for New Generations.* Grand Rapids: Zondervan, 2003.

LaCugna, Catherine M. *God for US: The Trinity and Christian Life.* San Francisco: Harper/Collins, 1991.

Levinson, Paul. *Digital McLuhan: A Guide to the Information Millennium.* London & New York: Routledge, 1999.

Loder, James E. *The Logic of the Spirit: Human Development in Theological Perspective.* San Francisco: Jossey-Bass, 1998.

Luhmann, Niklas. *Ecological Communication.* Translated by John Bednarz Jr. Cambridge, UK: Polity, 1986.

McFague, Sallie. *The Body of God: An Ecological Theology.* Minneapolis: Fortress, 1993.

McGrath, Alister E. *A Passion for Truth: The Intellectual Coherence of Evangelicalism.* Leicester, England: Apollos, 1996.

McKnight, Scot. *Turning to Jesus: The Sociology of Conversion in the Gospels.*

Louisville, KY: Westminster John Knox, 2002.
McLaren, Brian. *More Ready Than You Realize: Evangelism as Dance in the Postmodern Matrix.* Grand Rapids: Zondervan, 2002.
McLuhan, Marshall. *Understanding Media: The Extensions of Man.* New York: New American Library, 1964.
Milbank, John. "'Postmodern Critical Augustinianism': A Short Summa in Forty Two Responses to Unasked Questions." *Modern Theology* 7, no. 3 (April 1991): 225-37.
Miles, Margaret R. *The Word Made Flesh: A History of Christian Thought.* Malden, MA: Blackwell, 2005.
Mittelberg, Mark. *Building a Contagious Church: Revolutionizing the Way We View and Do Evangelism.* Grand Rapids: Zondervan, 2000.
Moen, Phyllis ed. *Examining Lives in Context: Perspectives on the Ecology of Human Development.* Washington DC: American Psychological Association, 1995.
Moltmann, Jürgen. *God in Creation: A New Theology of Creation and the Spirit of God.* Translated by Margaret Kohl. Minneapolis: Fortress, 1993.
_____. *The Trinity and the Kingdom.* Translated by Margaret Kohl. San Francisco: Harper and Row, 1981.
Myers, Joseph R. *The Search to Belong: Rethinking Intimacy, Community, and Small Groups.* Grand Rapids: Zondervan, 2003.
Ong, Walter. *Orality and Literacy: The Technologizing of the Word.* New York: Methuen, 1982.
Peace, Richard. *Conversion in the New Testament: Paul and the Twelve.* Grand Rapids: Eerdmans, 1999.
Peck, Scott M. *Further Along the Road Less Traveled: The Unending Journey Toward Spiritual Growth.* New York: Simon & Schuster, 1993.
Pembroke, Neil. *The Art of Listening: Dialogue, Shame and Pastoral Care.* Grand Rapids: Eerdmans, 2002.
Pickard, Stephen K. *Liberating Evangelism: Gospel Theology and the Dynamics of Communication.* Harrisburg, PA: Trinity Press International, 1999.
Pickstock, Catherine. *After Writing: On the Liturgical Consummation of Philosophy.* Malden, Mass.: Blackwell, 1998.
Poster, Mark. *The Second Media Age.* Cambridge, UK: Polity, 1995.
Postman, Neil. *Technopoly: The Surrender of Culture to Technology.* New York: Vintage, 1993.
Rainer, Thom S. *Surprising Insights from the Unchurched and Proven Ways to Reach Them.* Grand Rapids: Zondervan, 2001.
_____. *The Unchurched Next Door: Understanding Faith Stages as Keys to Sharing Your Faith.* Grand Rapids: Zondervan, 2003.
Rambo, Lewis. *Understanding Religious Conversion.* New Have, CT: Yale University Press, 1993.
Raynolds, Vernon and Ralph Tanner. *The Social Ecology of Religion.* New York: Oxford University, 1995.
Richardson, Rick. *Evangelism Outside the Box: New Ways to Help People*

Experience the Good News. Downers Grove, IL: InterVarsity Press, 2000.

Rieber, Robert ed. *The Individual, Communication, & Society.* Cambridge: Cambridge University Press, 1989.

Ritzer, George. *McDonaldization of Society.* Thousand Oaks, CA: Pine Forge, 1993.

_____. *The Globalization of Nothing.* Thousand Oaks, CA: Pine Forge, 2004.

Roof, Wade C. *A Generation of Seekers: The Spiritual Journey of the Baby Boom Generation.* New York: HarperCollins, 1993.

Rudnick, Milton L. *Speaking the Gospel through the Ages: A History of Evangelism.* St. Louis, MO: Concordia, 1984.

Rushkoff, Douglas. *Coercion: Why We Listen to What "They" Say.* New York: Riverhead, 1999.

Sample, Tex. *U.S. Lifestyles and Mainline Churches: A Key to Reaching People in the 90's.* Louisville, KY: Westminster/John Knox Press, 1990.

Santrock, John W. *Life-Span Development.* New York: McGraw-HIL, 2002.

Sardar, Ziauddin. *Postmodernism and the Other: The New Imperialism of Western Culture.* London and Chicago: Pluto, 1998.

Sargeant, Kimon H. *Seekeer Churches: Promoting Traditional Religion in a Nontraditional Way.* New Brunswick, NJ: Rutgers University, 2000.

Schaeffer, Edith. *The Hidden Art of Homemaking: Creative Ideas for Enriching Everyday Life.* Wheaton, Il: Tyndale House, 1971.

_____. *The Tapestry: The Life and Times of Francis and Edith Schaeffer.* Waco, TX: Word Books, 1981.

Schultz, Thom and Joani. *Why Nobody Learns Much of Anything at Church: and How to Fix It.* Loveland, CO: Group, 1993.

Schultze, Quentin J. *Communicating for Life: Christian Stewardship in Community and Media.* Grand Rapids, MI: Baker Books, 1999.

_____. *Habits of the High-Tech Heart: Living Virtuously in the Information Age.* Grand Rapids: Baker, 2002.

Schwarz, Christian A. *Natural Church Development: A Guide to Eight Essential Qualities of Healthy Churches.* Carol Stream, IL: Church Smart Resources, 1996.

Sider, Ronald J. *Cup of Water Bread of Life: Inspiring Stories about Overcoming Lopsided Christianity.* Grand Rapids: Zondervan, 1994.

Sider, Ronald J., Philip N. Olson & Heidi R. Unruh. *Churches That Make a Difference: Reaching Your Community with Good News and Good Works.* Grand Rapids: Baker, 2002.

Smith, Gordon. *Beginning Well: Christian Conversion & Authentic Transformation.* Downers Grove, IL: InterVarsity Press, 2001.

Smiths, James. *Speech and Theology: Language and the Logic of Incarnation.* New York: Routledge, 2002.

Snyder, Howard and Daniel V. Runyon. *Decoding the Church: Mapping the DNA of Christ's Body.* Grand Rapids: Baker, 2002.

St. John of Damascus, *On the Divine Image: Three Apologies Against Those Who Attack the Divine Images,* trans. David Anderson (Crestwood, NY: St.

Vladimir's Seminary Press, 1980

Stark, Rodney and Roger Finke. *Acts of Faith: Explaining the Human Side of Religion.* Berkley and Los Angeles: University of California Press, 2000.

Stark, Rodney. *The Rise of Christianity: How the Obscure, Marginal Jesus Movement Became the Dominant Religious Force in the Western World in a Few Centuries.* Princeton, NJ: HarperCollins, 1997.

Steinke, Peter L. *Healthy Congregations: A Systems Approach.* Bethesda, MD: Alban Institute, 1993.

Stephen Hunt, *Anyone for Alpha: Evangelism in a Post-Christian Society* (London: Darton, Longman, and Todd, 2001).

Stephens, Mitchell. *The Rise of the Image and the Fall of the Word.* New York: Oxford University Press, 1998.

Struass, William and Neil Howe. *Generations: The History of America's Future, 1584 to 2069.* New York: William Morrow and Company, 1990.

Tanner, Kathryn. *Theories of Culture: A New Agenda for Theology.* Minneapolis: Fortress, 1997.

Tillich, Paul. *A Theology of Culture.* London: Oxford University Press, 1959.

_____. *Systematic Theology.* Vol. II. Chicago: The University of Chicago Press, 1967.

Ward, Peter. "Alpha – the McDonaldization of Religion?" *ANVIL* Vol. 15 (No 4, 1998).

White, Daniel. *Postmodern Ecology: Communication, Evolution, and Play.* Albany, NY: State University of New York Press, 1998.

Willimon, William. *The Gospel for the Person Who Has Everything.* Valley Forge, PA: Judson Press, 1978.

Willis, Paul. *Common Culture: Symbolic Work at Play in the Everyday Cultures of the Young.* Milton Keynes, England: Open University Press, 1990.

Wuthnow, Robert. *After Heaven: Spirituality in America Since the 1950s.* Berkeley and Los Angeles: University of California Press, 1989.

_____. *All In Sync: How Music and Art Are Revitalizing American Religion.* Berkeley: University of California Press, 2003.

www.ingramcontent.com/pod-product-compliance
Lightning Source LLC
Chambersburg PA
CBHW051945160426
43198CB00013B/2303